AMERICA'S
LEADING
LADIES
WHO POSITIVELY IMPACT OUR WORLD

Laleh Alemzadeh-Hancock	Dr. Alison Parker Henderson
Deborah Armstrong	Cynthia Higgins, MD
Mary T. Barra	Maria Horstmann
Debra Ann Bartz	Michaelee Jenkins
Marta Brummell	Celeste Johnson-Matheson
Nicole Caley	Shelley Joy
Geneviève Carle	Lori Kessler
Mallika Chopra	Ingrid Laederach-Steven
Traci Clarida	Marie-Flore Lindor-Latortue
Mary Clement, ND	Kathryn R. Martin
Anita R. Minor Clifford	Jennifer Milner
Ortell Diane Cromer	Marium Murad, MD
Demetria Davenport	Natalie Rekstad
Tonja Demoff	Virginia Rometty
Eileen DiFrancesco, MD	Pat Sampson
Rhonda Maria Farrah	Marjorie Saulson
Jory H. Fisher	Dawn C. Sequeira, Esq.
Cordelia Gaffar	Lancia Soans
Cindy Galvin	Tina Tehranchian
Melinda Gates	Paula Neva Vail
Natalie W. Geary, MD	Renee Villanova
Geri Gibbons	Ana Weber
Catherine Gruener	Leah M. Williams
Carolyn Stowers Harris	Oprah Winfrey
Claudia Harvey	Jenny Xu
Anita Hawkins	

"Think like a queen. A queen is not afraid to fail. Failure is another steppingstone to greatness." ~ Oprah Winfrey

STRONG WOMEN
aren't simply born.

We are forged through the challenges of life. With each challenge we grow mentally and emotionally.

We move forward with our head held high and a strength that can not be denied. A woman who's been through the storm and survived.

We Are Warriors!

The Power of Storytelling

THIS is the moment in time to shine the light on the hopes, dreams, and positive visions of our personal and collective life experiences. *How?* Stories. Storytelling is at the heart of how we communicate. Love is the guiding force. *We are all* ONE, *connected with each other in a very deep and powerful way.*

Together let's celebrate America's Leading Ladies ~ incredible strong women many of whom are universally recognized, women who inspire us all, who followed their passion and with drive, dedication, discipline and persistence set out to do something they love and reached the top pillars of success in their personal and professional lives.

Let love in. Let these ladies remind us of how much goodness there is in this world. *Connect* with who you truly are and with people who make you feel deeply. Learn how these role-models became positive Influencers in a world that needs voices of strong women heard. *By opening hearts and minds and sharing experiences they contribute greatly to our sense of connection.* They encourage us to aim high, speak our heart's truth, and release self-imposed limitations on what we think we could do or become. *That's what great stories do.*

To love what you do and feel that it matters breeds optimism and feelings of well-being. *Brush off the dust of doubt.* There's a big, wonderful world out there. Each one of us has a role to play to make the world more caring and compassionate that transcends "you" and "me", "us" and "them". In that light, we added stories of awesome Leading Ladies from Canada, Iran, Mexico, India, and the United Kingdom.

ALL have great stories to tell. And that's something ~ to be thankful for ~ especially in these moments of great unrest ~ to shine a spotlight as a beacon of hope on the journeys of strong, passionate and compassionate women who make this world a better place. Read On.

DEDICATION

America's Leading Ladies (ALL) gratefully dedicates this book to Ruth Bader Ginsberg, Supreme Court Associate Justice, (nicknamed "Notorious RBG" by her biographers and followers). As a young lawyer, her early legal battles changed the world for women.

*Ruth Bader Ginsberg
Associate Justice of the Supreme
Court of the United States*

Considered the legal architect of the modern women's rights movement, she fought for eliminating gender discrimination of both females and males - enshrined in American Law - becoming an unexpected pop culture icon. What emerges is an inspiring portrait of a woman in the highest court in the land who helped expand the concept of *"equal justice for all."*

What makes her life story even more compelling is that, at 85, she is embracing her popularity as another tool in her effort to help women advance, and which means so much to young women. As Gloria Steinman states: *"I can't tell you how happy it makes me to see her name on campus T-shirts as the Notorious RBG. A majority consciousness is finally catching up to where she's been all along."*

AMERICA'S LEADING LADIES (ALL)
Who Positively Impact Our World
© Copyright 2019 ALLPress. Global/ Pat Sampson
All Rights Reserved

Founder/ Editor: Pat Sampson
Interior Design/Layout: Eddie Egesi
Cover Design: Haris Čizmić
Quote Images: Joel Heron
Ebook Conversion: AtriTex Technologies

ALLPress.Global
Gaithersburg, Maryland 20878
ALLPress.Global@gmail.com
NetworkofStars11@gmail.com
www.NetworkofStars.us

Acknowledgements

"Choose people in your life who lift you up . . .
Who appreciate you . . . who give you hope."
-Michelle Obama

America's Leading Ladies(ALL) are awesome role models. Optimistic. Thought Provoking. Inspiring. Motivating. They teach us a thing or two about never backing down and also about giving back. Their stories shine a light on the superpower feminine spirit in action!

ALL loves the wonderful men who make a positive difference. Believing in gender equality, the next book will focus on the success stories and challenges men face and what keeps them going when setbacks occur.

Eddie Egesi: the incredibly talented Visual Artist who created the interior design and layout - worked tirelessly with endless revisions - and a positive attitude - committed to making this book as good as it could be. He succeeded. www.designsbyegesi.com

Haris Čizmić: Award Winning Creative Designer, Artist/Filmographer for his talent, insight, and unrelenting patience in producing the book cover that captures the essence of ALL. www.hariscizmic.com

Joel Heron: Great graphic designer with a winning attitude to match. My heartfelt thanks for her talent in designing the inspiring quotes and beautiful photographs into wonderful images seen throughout. www.Onlinedesignandsupportiveservices.com

AtriTex Technologies: Internationally acclaimed experts in Book Design and eBook Creation are adapt at taking any input and converting them into beautiful output files in different formats. I am grateful for their professional guidance and excellence as reflected throughout these pages. www.atritex.com

Houman "Dave" Taghipour: *As a kindred spirit, we share a real synchronicity. I learned so much from the keen understanding and sound perspective of this young, thoughtful, successful, and caring environmentalist, that he became a true compass and collaborator on this incredible journey.*

Tricia Walsh *and* **Lisa Sampson:** *My two beautiful, talented, and incredible daughters who have shown the smarts, strength and optimism to face life's challenges and win. I am so proud of all that you are and all you will become. I love you.*

Ryan Walsh: My beloved grandson's inspiring presence is missed every moment of every day. His awesome attitude and positive outlook inspired all who came across his path. He will forever be remembered in the hearts and minds of all the lives he touched.

John dela Vega: The loss of a life-long close friend is tough to bear. His influence on my life is immeasurable. His legacy as one of the nation's most revered portrait painters, playwright, author, teacher, man of love and compassion will live on for generations to come.

Mary Clement, Ingrid Laederach Steven, Rhonda Maria Farrah, Sandy Taylor, Paula Permison and Lancia Soans, my true friends. They have the faith in me that comes only in true friendship, and the kind of friendship, once it comes, never goes away.

And, as always, my love and gratitude to every person who has come into my life for a reason, a season, or a lifetime.

I would love to hear from all the Leading Ladies, whose stories are yet to be told. Networkofstars11@gmail.com

Love, Light, Peace, Joy, to Everyone, Everywhere!

Pat Sampson

> **"** I'm grateful
> to be a woman.
> There's something
> which impels us
> to show our
> inner souls.
> The more
> courageous
> we are,
> the more
> we succeed
> in explaining
> what we
> know. **"**
>
> - *Maya Angelou*

CONTENTS

Every individual
matters.
Every individual
has a role to play.
Every individual
makes a difference.

-Jane Goodall

Oprah Winfrey

Founder, Oprah Winfrey

Leadership Academy for Girls

Photograph Courtesy of Harpo, Inc./ Chris Craymer

Oprah Winfrey

BIOGRAPHY

Oprah Winfrey is a global media leader, philanthropist, producer and actress. She has created an unparalleled connection with people around the world, making her one of the most respected and admired figures today.

For 25 years, Winfrey was host and producer of the award-winning talk show *"The Oprah Winfrey Show."* In her role as Chairman and CEO of *OWN: Oprah Winfrey Network*, she's guiding her cable network to success. Winfrey is the founder of *O, The Oprah Magazine* and oversees *Harpo Films*. In 2017, Winfrey debuted her first segment as a *CBS Minutes Special Correspondent.*

Winfrey is an Academy Award-nominated actress for her role in *"The Color Purple,"* earned critical acclaim in *"Lee Daniels' The Butler"* and produced and acted in the Academy Award-winning film *"Selma."* Winfrey starred in the Emmy nominated HBO Films *"The Immortal Life of Henrietta Lacks"* and most recently portrayed *"Mrs. Which"* in Disney's *"Wrinkle in Time"* film adaptation from director Ava DuVernay.

In 2015, Winfrey joined the Weight Watchers board of directors. In 2017, Winfrey launched a new refrigerated food line *"O, That's Good"* featuring soups and sides that bring a nutritious twist on comfort food classics using real ingredients and no artificial flavors or dyes in collaboration with Kraft Heinz. Ten percent of the profits are equally split between charitable organizations *Rise Against Hunger* and *Feeding America* to support the fight against hunger.

In 2017, her cookbook *"Food, Health and Happiness: 115 On Point Recipes for Great Meals and a Better Life"* and *"Wisdom of Sundays"* both debuted as #1 on the New York Times Bestsellers List under her personal book imprint *"An Oprah Book."*

During a December 2002 visit with Nelson Mandela, she pledged to build a school in South Africa and has contributed more than $140 million towards providing education for academically gifted girls from disadvantaged backgrounds. Graduates of the school have continued on to higher education both in South Africa and at colleges and universities around the world.

In 2013, Winfrey was awarded the Medal of Freedom, the nation's highest civilian honor.

Top 10 Rules for Success

by Oprah Winfrey

"Do the work that comes from your soul."

The single greatest wisdom I think I've ever received is that the key to fulfillment, success, happiness, contentment in life is when you align your personality with what your soul actually came to do. I believe everyone has a soul and their own personal spiritual energy. When you use your personality to serve whatever that thing is, you can't help but be successful.

1. Understand the next right move.

The biggest adventure you can take is to live the life of your dreams. How do you know what the next right move is? You sit still and ask yourself, *'What is the next right move? What is the next right move?'* and then, from that space, make the next right move and the next right move.

2. Seize your opportunity.

Nothing about my life is lucky. Nothing. A lot of grace, a lot of blessings, a lot of divine order, but I don't believe in luck. For me, luck is preparation meeting the moment of opportunity. There is no luck without you being prepared to handle that moment of opportunity. Every single thing that has ever happened in your life is preparing you for the moment that is to come.

3. Everyone makes mistakes.

Wherever you are in your journey, I hope you, too, will keep encountering challenges. It is a blessing to be able to survive them, to be able to keep putting one foot in front of the other – to be in a position to make the climb up life's mountain, knowing that the summit still lies ahead. And every experience is a valuable teacher.

4. Work on Yourself.

The world has so many lessons to teach you. I consider the world, this Earth, to be like a school and our life the classrooms. And sometimes here in this Planet Earth school the lessons often come dressed up as detours or roadblocks. And sometimes as full-blown crises. And the secret I've learned to getting ahead is being open to the lessons, lessons from the grandest university of all, that is, the universe itself.

5. Run the race as hard as you can.

Don't waste your time in the race looking back to see what the other guy is doing. It's not about the other guy. It's about what can you do. You just need to run that race as hard as you can. You need to give it everything you've got, all the time, for yourself.

6. Believe.

You don't become what you want. You become what you believe. Stop the crazy mind chatter in your head that tells you all the time that you are not good enough. Do the one thing you think you cannot do. Fail at it. Try again. Do better the second time. The only people who never tumble are those who never mount the high wire. This is your moment. Own it.

7. We are all seeking the same thing.

When you make loving others the story of your life, there's never a final chapter, because the legacy continues. You lend your light to one person, and he or she shines it on another and another and another. And I know for sure that in the final analysis of our lives -when the to-do lists are no more, when the frenzy is finished, when our e-mail inboxes are empty - the only thing that will have any lasting value is whether we've loved others and whether they've loved us.

8. Find your purpose.

You have to find what sparks a light in you so that you in your own way can illuminate the world. It's what you feel. It is the thing that gives you juice. The thing that you are supposed to do. And nobody can tell you what that is. You know it inside yourself.

9. Stay grounded.

It is ALL that really matters ... when you surrender, and stop resisting, and stop trying to change that which you cannot change, but be in the moment, be fully open to the blessings you have already received, and those that are yet to come to you, and stand in that space of gratitude, and honor, and claim that for yourself, and look at where you are, and how far you have come, and what you've gotten, and what you've accomplished, and who you are.

10. Relax, it's going to be okay.

Relax, relax. It's going to be OK. It's really going to be OK. You are more capable than you can even imagine. Trust yourself and in your capacity to know what is right for you. And then find a way to offer it to others in the form of service, working hard, and also allowing the energy of the universe to lead you.

* * *

Oprah Winfrey
OPRAH.com

Claudia Harvey

Business Woman, Inventor
Speaker & Philanthropist

BIOGRAPHY

Claudia Harvey is a force of nature. Businesswoman, inventor, investor, international speaker, author, philanthropist and proud Mother of three. She chose to live life on her own terms when, in 2009, boot-strapped her first business to international success and never looked back! She left her successful 20+ year corporate career behind and started her first business venture **Dig It®Apparel Inc**. It wasn't long before Claudia became an international motivator sharing her story of personal strategic choices that evolved into stepping stones of growth and great success.

It started with an idea and a pair of gloves! Dig It® created a revolutionary product never before seen in the world. It received national exposure when Claudia successfully struck a deal with venture capitalist Kevin O'Leary of CBC's Dragons' Den and NBC's Shark Tank fame. Dig It® has realized considerable international retail growth, adding new products, and launching a new product line, **Dig My Life™**, in 2019.

Within a few short years, Claudia transformed herself from "*pitcher*" to "*investor*" in other people's businesses, as well as providing valuable insight and guidance to help create growth through personal, business and financial empowerment.

A contributing author of three #1 International Best Selling Books, Claudia inspires, empowers, and helps others maximize their potential. Creating a life where there is balance between a thriving career and raising a family, gives Claudia valuable insights and life-lessons to share as a sought-after speaker. She inspires audiences world-wide along with other international Influencers: Tony Robbins, Mark Victor Hansen, Jim Treliving, Pitbull, and many more notables in their field.

Claudia was recently awarded **"Top Business Professional 2019"** by the International Association of Top Professionals. Aside from her illustrious career, Claudia assists organizations dedicated to empowering women and youth, such as **Sonas.org**, whose mandate is to create sustainable social enterprise to employ, feed, clothe and educate women and their families. Claudia established a scholarship funded with proceeds received from selling Sonas.org organic-made products in North America.

21

SUCCESS
... YOURS TO DEFINE

by Claudia Harvey

> *"The pessimist sees difficulty in every opportunity.*
> *The optimist sees opportunity in every difficulty."*
> *-- Winston Churchill*

We ALL are a product of nature and nurture. The circumstances we are born into, opportunities presented and taken, unique experiences that create our history and patterns, combine to form who we are, what we desire, what we can handle, and what we *want* to handle, shapes our destiny. These decisions significantly impact our financial and emotional foundation and most importantly, creates a ripple effect on our experiences that impact our lives and those around us.

We can find ourselves as a reflection of others, not living the life we truly desire, until a moment in time an epiphany occurs, that makes us take stock of our present reality. This awakening can positively impact the next course of action we take, or stop us like a deer in headlights, retreating to what is comfortable and familiar but allowing no opportunity for growth.

The first step to changing a pattern that no longer serves you is recognizing that your inner voice is speaking to you. The next step is stopping to really listen to it. The third step is taking action. Taking action can be immensely difficult as outside forces and influences can be so great you feel "forced" to retreat to established patterns and resist growth. We often retreat because **HOW** gets in the way. We fear the uncertain. We fear the judgement of others. We fear failure. However, "failure should be redefined as a learning experience, and recognized as opportunities for growth and self-empowerment. We fear the word "no". Most of us heard the word "no" as infants and we managed to circumvent and grow despite obstacles put in our path.

I was blessed by recognizing some epiphanies as they occurred. I would stop and listen to my inner voice asking me to take stock of what I was doing: and how were my current actions serving my purpose? Or, could I make better *choices* to ensure living the life I truly wanted to live? I made the dramatic conscious choice of leaving behind a career that the outside world deemed "successful" ; a career I had nurtured all of my adult life and *thought* I desired from age 10.

I grew up as a child of immigrant parents who survived the post-war and depression era. We lived a frugal life, but my brother and I had an abundance of encouragement and support. My parents' philosophy was "work hard and save". They believed that the harder you worked, the more successful you became. Financial security was paramount to their way of thinking, and earning money the definition of success.

I worked hard as I was taught but lost what was important to me. The impact of my unhappy reality crashed into my heart and soul one gray February day, while struggling through Chicago O'Hare Airport carrying coats, bags, a computer, and miscellaneous necessities required for my "successful"life. **Why?** So I could attend one meeting after another, farther and farther away from my young family with every passing day. I collapsed exhausted into the plane seat, and like a lightning bolt-it struck me! I was living my parents' definition of success... *not my own!*

It was important to me ... *living a life with strength, balance and harmony*. At that moment, I reflected on the years I trained, educated, and supported my current path ... for **WHAT?** I wasn't *happy*. And further, how would I redefine what this elusive definition of "*happiness*" was? I had two choices ... keep living on this treadmill to simply survive and meet the expectation of others' definition of success? **OR** take stock of how to live on my own terms and strategically decide how to change course!

We live in a society where immediate gratification is paramount; where we can "uber-ask" for almost anything instantaneously. I knew that to create long-lasting change often takes considerable effort and patience, and the **HOW** can get lost in the noise and demands of everyday life.

Discover your **HOW** by implementing the following five steps.

1. Surround yourself with those that lift up your spirit.

Is your network of close friends and associates celebrating personal victories, acquiring new skills, and conquering new adventures? Are you equally motivated to do the same? Anyone we spend time with influences our behavior by their attitudes and conversation. Do these conversations lift you up or leave you feeling deflated by self-doubt? Minimize your exposure to unsupportive and often toxic-relationships and soon you will attract more positive, enlightened people into your orbit who support your dreams and encourage your growth.

2. Do what makes you happy, then do it again.

Sounds simple, doesn't it? But really, I challenge you to think about it. What makes you truly, deep-seated happy? Do you remember a moment of pure bliss and excitement? Did you experience a moment when you felt complete? How old were you? What were you doing? How long did it last? Whatever that moment was, *rinse and repeat*. That moment of happiness feels like balm to our soul, a mini-mindset vacation to regroup and set aside daily stresses. Allow yourself to feel joy. Accept that it's ok to take time to carve out special moments for yourself. Go where the happy happenings are. Sing songs that inspire you. Go where the good words are being spoken. Travel with people who are productive and inspired. Speak positively of yourself and others. Say a good word on behalf of life and you can expect it to return the favor.

Focus on the end game.

Once your goal is lit brightly enough by the fire of your imagination to see it clearly, let nothing real, or imagined sway you off course. Like the Nike slogan, **"Just do it"**, focus on your cherished goal and each day move one step toward its fulfillment. One forward action *every day*, turns into 365 steps in one year! Imagine how far you'll come! As you gain experience, each step becomes easier, creating a more positive outcome, as the realization of your heart's desire becomes more tangible. Each flicker of disappointment is actually a spark of hope to ignite the physical, intellectual, emotional, and spiritual strength that drives personal achievement that, in turn, inspires others to follow your example.

4. Live life in gratitude.

You walk out your door free to follow the dreams of your heart. Nothing is too much to put into your thoughts, or put into your day. We all have "hard" days, of course. Obstacles appear on our path to challenge us. I specifically use "hard day" not "bad day" because the power of language sets the tone of a positive mindset that impacts your ultimate goals. I begin every day with a conscious thought of thankfulness... and list all the things for which I am grateful. I end each day listing two to three things that happened for which I am thankful. This can be as small as arriving home ten minutes earlier than expected, or the sun peeked out of the clouds, or my child gave me an extra long unexpected hug, or I met someone that day I believe will positively impact my life. Find a positive moment or two in your life, amplify it, acknowledge it, and life becomes more positive and fulfilling promising bright tomorrows!

5. Believe you have the power of choice.

It is a natural tendency to cling to the familiar, but growth is impossible without change. Be confident. Be expectant of grand and beautiful results from everything you do. You are blessed to live in a society of abundance, free to choose and create a path that fits your own personal definition of success. The opportunity to choose your life's path, despite challenges along the way, is one of the most rewarding experiences you can have. Have you ever been asked to do something, go to an event, or meet someone you really didn't want to, but you *did* and that one circumstance changed the course of your life? *Think about it.* Consider everything, but be positive and welcome the feelings of natural excitement that travel with change.

You can read these words, choose to settle back into your comfort zone because it's easy, comfortable, and familiar. **OR**, you can make the dedicated decision to make the changes you truly desire. Choose to take steps to make it happen. Decide on your goal and reverse engineer the steps needed. And if you find yourself challenged to create the right strategy, find others that can help support your dream and goals ... and go back to the first *HOW: Surround yourself with those that lift up your spirit!*

* * *

Claudia Harvey
info@claudiaharvey.com
www.claudiaharvey.com

Anita Hawkins

Model, Author
Philanthropist & Producer

Anita Hawkins

BIOGRAPHY

Anita Hawkins, entrepreneur extraordinaire succeeds at whatever she sets out to accomplish. Anita, abundant in beauty and business know-how, has walked the runway of high-profile fashion events & designers.

Anita grew up in Gary, Indiana. Although a teen mom, her passion and desire to be an entrepreneur, birthed when she inherited her grandmother's hair salon. This gift impelled Anita to hone her skills as a licensed cosmetologist, enabling her to grow her clientele in-house and through personal visits, blossomed into a successful thriving business. **This was the beginning for the young woman with big dreams.**

In 2000, Anita married Major League Baseball pitcher, LaTroy Hawkins, after relocating to Texas. In 2011 she founded Trokar Industries, LLC., to acquire numerous land developments around the state. Propelled on the path of successful business ventures and a life altering event (diagnosed with a rare blood disorder) Anita carved out critical lifestyle changes that included healthy foods and exercise. She aquired the Fresh Healthy Café Franchise, receiving the master designation title for Dallas/Ft. Worth.

Anita has been recognized by the National Association of Professional Women for Outstanding Excellence and Dedication to her Profession and the Advancement of Women, and was awarded the President's Philanthropy Award from Women of Wealth Magazine.

Following the adage **"to whom much is given, much is required,"** Anita and her husband, champion various philanthropic causes. "The Jackie Robinson Foundation" sponsors college education of deserving students to the school of their choice. "Women Called Moses," and "Find One Reason to Smile," serves as safe homes for women and children fleeing domestic abuse. Anita is on the Planning Committee, and walks annually in support of St. Jude's Hospital, consistently one of their top fund raisers. In her debut novel **"The Storm After the Storm."** Anita chronicles her rise from the depths of abuse, anger and despair to triumph, self-love, and success in her business and personal life.

Mastering You
by Anita Eloise Hawkins

"Every storm is bringing you closer to your destiny."

Everybody has a story, and everyone experiences storms, myself included. I look at storms as wildfires. Wildfires aren't always negative. If we see them the right way, the storms of our lives have purpose. We just need to learn how to master ourselves, so we can master our storms.

Learning how to see beyond your issues is difficult, because you want the fires to go out and the storms resolved. Ultimately, what's true and righteous, regardless of what anyone may think, is middleground where everything makes sense. The ground where, after a storm blows over, new life begins - coming from a place of truth.

Mastering You

I came to a point in life where all the storms I faced tied me up in knots. So, I made time to really look at myself and those things important to me.

I began by coming to terms with who I am and what I believe. I had to know what believing really meant for me. I came to understand that my most important partners were my core values, the deepest part of what I believed to be true and right. And, of course, that begin with God, -- you have to believe in something - and He is the source of all things. Then I focused on believing in myself, and the good intentions of others.

I recognized that belief is a heartfelt acceptance: faith, trust, and certainty that you are here for a reason and have a unique purpose to fill. It's knowing every storm is bringing you closer to your unique destiny. Believing ignites your passion. It builds assurance and confidence. It is an anchor that releases vision, intuition, and your best innate abilities. I feel that to believe is to be loved. On a spiritual level, I view it as getting what's mine, knowing that my maximum value is everything that I need.

Mastering Your Life

Life is all about seeing things for what they are now and redefining them- it all starts with reinventing you. I call this **'Loving Myself to Life'.** Loving who I am in the skin I'm in. Accepting me for me - a work in progress. We each need to accept who we really are, being aware we all have dysfunctional areas. No-one is perfect. So, we need to own who we are completely, including our imperfections, as we keep flowing through life's storms.

Be a willing participant in the process and see everything through to completion, no matter what wildfires appear. Be willing to cope with the challenges and you'll not only put the fire out, you'll fulfill your purpose along the way.

My balance is my center. I've learned how to balance spirituality, health and wellness, love and relationships, and finances. Putting feet to what I believe is something I have to keep learning every day. I'm sure you relate.

When you talk about balancing everything in your life, you are the ruler of the conversation. You rule it by owning it, or everything falls apart. God helps you take control and bring balance into your world. Dare to live on full overflow. When storms and wildfires rage around you, be a help in your own rescue.

You need to stand on your story, not in your story, As you stand on your story you'll be able to say, "This is what happened to me, and this is how I got through it."You'll be able to help others find their way to safety. Make sure you're standing on a strong foundation. Be firmly rooted in who you are and what you want in life. Be intentional and take action. Breakdowns occur from unfulfilled expectations. They happen when people say or do things to us that we don't understand. So, in everything, master you and everything else will follow.

Loving yourself to life!

Excellence is attainable. Work hard to achieve and manage it. It's a step-by-step, day-to-day process. Each day do something toward mastering you. Growth comes in levels. We have to continually perfect who we are. If we don't, we become stagnant, while everybody else is growing. There's always room for growth and why our wildfires have purpose. That's why the sun comes up and brings a beautiful new day after a storm. In this life, we never fully arrive.

Your holistic wealth reveals who you are in the dark of night. It also determines what legacy you are leaving for those who come after you. I learned that 15% of what we do is based on our vocation and 85% on foundation, strategy and relationships. This is why we must learn to love ourselves to life, to value others and to master everything we do. Then when storms and wildfires arrive, they won't destroy us.

The process of transformation takes time. Very few things happen overnight. We live in a microwave generation. Everyone wants everything fast. I have discovered that I need to be 'slow-cooked'. That way, my life gets "seasoned" better. Microwaved food doesn't taste as good, just as quick fixes don't usually work out. Join me in the 'slow-cooker'?

Finally, I tell my daughter that no matter what storm arrives, whether family issues or some other hardship, find one thing a day to make you happy. Yes, one thing can do it! When you awaken, be happy you opened your eyes and regained consciousness. That's the first thing. Then tomorrow, be happy you can see. The next day, be grateful you can hear. The fourth day, celebrate your ability to think clearly. On the fifth day be happy you can walk. You see? Five days of the week, covered! Each ritual simple, but needed to survive and thrive. And literally Thousands of things can make us happy! **Count your blessings!**

You may not have everything you want, nor everything you need, but you do have a lot to be thankful for and think about. Don't take anything for granted. Your current mindset is leading you to your experience. If you have a mindset that you are not getting anywhere that's where your experience will lead you - nowhere. Your mindset has to be positive, moving, growing, changing and transforming your future.

'The Storm After The Storm'

Storms can be violent, even tragic, but they don't have to define you. You have only one life, one story, so choose to master the negative things. Look objectively at these things and think, "What good can I turn this into?" Then take action and turn the negatives into positives. The law of attraction will be working in your favor as you love yourself to life and claim your own greatness.

No matter what you may have suffered or lost in the storms of life, there's a purpose for positivity in everything. A new day always comes, and new life can rise out of the ashes. Be yourself and stand on your storms. Commit yourself fully to reinventing and mastering you; letting go of any attachments that no longer serve you. Don't let anything you do be just for the moment. Be committed to making everything you do count for a lifetime.

Start each day by looking far out into the horizon. Know who you are. Know what you want. Do what it takes to achieve your goals. Strive to be happy. As you master your storms, an abundance of possibilities lay before you.

* * *

Anita Hawkins
FindOneReasonToSmile@gmail.com
www.findonereasontosmile.org
www.AnitaEHawkins.com

Jennifer Milner

CEO, Panache Management

Entrepreneur
Model and Talent Manager

Jennifer Milner

BIOGRAPHY

Entrepreneur extraordinaire and source of inspiration to many, Jennifer Milner is chief executive officer of Panache Management, a hugely successful, international model and talent agency. An unfailingly positive visionary, Jennifer led the way of transforming the traditional modeling and talent business into one of inclusiveness. Her clients' self-esteem and careers flourished under her supportive guidance. Over the course of her career, Jennifer has received many awards and accolades. Recent awards include *2018 Top Model and Talent Manager of the Year*. Nominated for *2019 Business Innovator of the Year, Empowered Woman of the year and the Lifetime Achievement Award* by the *International Association of Top Professionals* (IATOP). Jennifer's success is truth layered with love, light, strength and courage. For Milner, it is never too early or too late to be your best self.

Founded in 1985, Panache has offices in Los Angeles and Canada, representing over 2,000 models and actors. The top Panache talent walks *Chanel, St. Laurent* and *Versace* runways, they model *Hugo Boss, Dsquared2* and shine in *Shiseido* campaigns. Panache models pose in *Abercrombe & Fitch* campaigns for superstar photographer Bruce Weber, gracing magazine covers and editorials for *Vogue, Elle, Harper's Bazaar GQ, Nylon, Shape* and numerous publications. A Panache model was the European face of *Wonderbra* for three years. Panache models represent haircare for *Schwarzkopf*. Panache's reach extends to Hollywood; hundreds of Panache clients have booked hit shows; *13 Reasons Why, American Horror Story, Blackish, Breaking Bad, Criminal Minds, Fargo, Game of Thrones, Grey's Anatomy, NCIS, Outlander, Ray Donovan, Riverdale, Stranger Things, Supernatural, The Walking Dead, This is Us, Veep and Westworld.*

Jennifer's presented diversity to their advertising clients well before it was 'fashionable' or 'mandatory.' Her stance on fair treatment and equal opportunities sparked a revolution in the modeling industry, transforming what society deems beautiful, and opening the door to new cultural, gender and size role models.

Doing the Right Thing
... for the Right Reasons

by Jennifer Milner

*"You and your purpose in life are the same thing.
Your purpose is to be you."*

The business of modeling and actor management is demanding and layered; at first glance it looks very glamorous but the challenges I witnessed in my early agency career inspired my personal mission as a responsible manager. Panache took the lead in ethical management practices, providing safe environments for young models and encouraging unique beauty.

With the understanding that unique looks tell a story that intrigues consumers at every level, fashion and advertising clients began to listen, and Panache's insistence on inclusiveness proved to be good for business. It was the right thing at the right time. I embraced the challenge of breaking the practices that needed to change in the industry. My approach was to strengthen and mentor talent from the inside out, helping models and actors to expand themselves past the boundaries defined by looks and beauty. Panache provides a complete environment of support, also offering a range of production services, including photographic shoots and artistic direction for fashion events. Panache talent is held to a high standard of professionalism, and as a result, our talent is in demand, working in major cities including Los Angeles, New York, Miami, Milan, Paris, Hamburg, London and Tokyo, As CEO, I maintain direct communication with our clients to keep them engaged with our evolving mission of innovation, inclusion and enlightenment. I impress upon our models and actors that their powerful thoughts and actions count.

This is a movement, and they are a part of my movement. I'm working hard to change the industry. I tell them often: "You are going to find people out there who are going to think that

35

you are perfect and that you shouldn't change one little thing about yourself. Your physical reality is irrelevant." **I encourage my talent to focus on more profound things including spirituality, volunteering and contributing to important causes.**

Dare to be 'Your Best You.'

My years in the business of representing talent have revealed certain unwavering truths on the path to success. I want to share this with you to be you - *your best self.*

> *"Always challenge yourself to show up with courage, determination, consistency and accountability to yourself, your process and your career."*

The path to find your *'inner you'* is easier for some than for others, but I promise you, it is a valuable and crucial career and life skill to cultivate. Tests of courage and determination present themselves in life and we all have things to overcome along the way. Once conquered, they activate the power of accomplishment, something that can never be taken away.

Everyone has different fears; we all experience them in our lives. Consistency and accountability helps build discipline and strength to face inner fears. When you are authentically meeting the challenge with your best efforts, self-love increases. Take time to discover the inner you and to recognize those traits as *uniquely you.*

Being who you are - the very best version of you - is the way to fulfillment, happiness, success and your true purpose in life. The depth of your personality holds the clues to your best self. What interests are you naturally drawn to? Allow that to externalize as you find yourself. *Embrace that* to be who you really are and to take risks. *Dare to be strong.* Be brave. Be authentic. Dare to inspire. You don't need to 'fit in.' Before overthinking things about how to 'do it right' or trying to guess what agents and casting directors seek, *find you first* and believe in yourself. They seek you. They want you - your authentic, inspired humanity. Always challenge yourself to show up with your personal brand of courage, determination, consistency and accountability. Keep learning about what interests you. Go deeper. Surprise yourself. Stand in possibility.

Believe in You. You need to believe in yourself before anything else. Begin with your belief in everything you find positive; let your strength rise from that. Accept the fact that you too can change the world. I am telling you from personal experience -- you have what it takes. Adopting the right attitude can convert any experience into a [more] positive one. Don't linger in disappointment. Pick yourself up from any challenges; face everything with a positive mindset knowing that you must live up to who you truly are.

Have Faith in Possibility. What you aspire to is possible. This is your *'best you'* rising to the challenge of the dream and your goals. Believe that you can do it regardless of what anyone says or where you are in life. You could encounter people who might say things that make you feel you are not enough. Have faith in possibility. You are enough.

Embrace Your Voice. In the very opinionated fashion/entertainment industry, people sometimes get lost or overpowered by the voice of others. This is especially true of young talent in dealings with seasoned agents and directors. You must own your voice and stand up with your opinion anytime, anywhere, with courage, respect and authenticity. Your strong presence deserves to be seen, your unique voice, in a professional expression of positivity, determination and accountability, deserves to be heard.

Let Go of Fear. This is really important. Don't allow fear to prevent you from finding the joy that comes in a life lived with courage. It should never rule or control your decisions. You are much stronger than your fear, you are more powerful than what you feel or think.

In fact, you are greater than you envision yourself. To lose fear, you must replace it with belief. Lay out your clear vision, believe and visualize it, and map out a strategy to achieve your goals. If you can't quite get this started alone, call upon a loved one to support you in this vision. Allow them to lend their strength of belief for you until you can find this on your own.

Visualize. Think deeply about what your life would look like if you had already achieved your dream. Live as if it is real. Put your whole self into it and let this reflect in how you relate with yourself and others.

Take action. You have to work toward your goals; no one is going to do that for you. It's not enough to visualize, you must work, applying the steps I've outlined. It begins inside as you get real with you, embrace your strength, find clarity, lose fear, visualize and plan the steps to secure what you truly want to achieve. It's the series of actions, the layers of foundation outlined that get you to this moment of your truth. Using your courage, overcoming challenges, embracing your voice, releasing fear, visualizing what you truly desire and applying it with determined action until you have achieved it, you will arrive.

Success is Achieved through Overcoming Challenges. As a newcomer into any industry, at any stage of life, you must remember the fact that no path is ever without challenges. Yes, you will fail at some point, but you must never give up. As long as you have goals and dreams in your soul, you are intended for greater things than you are doing at the present moment.

* * *

Jennifer Milner, CEO
Panache Management
Los Angeles & Canada
www.panachemanagement.com

Natalie Rekstad

Philanthropist

Founder and CEO
Black Fox Philanthropy, LLC, B Corp

Natalie Rekstad

BIOGRAPHY

Natalie Rekstad leads a purpose-driven life as the Founder and CEO of Black Fox Philanthropy, a leading fundraising strategy firm that exists to accelerate the social sector's effectiveness in solving complex problems on a global scale. As a B Corp, Black Fox Philanthropy measures the triple bottom line of people, planet, and profit.

Natalie's core belief is that the future hinges upon a more just and gender balanced world. She is a sought after panelist, speaker, and resource for a variety of organizations and universities on the topic of philanthropy, the social sector, and fundraising. She has been featured in dozens of local and national media outlets including CBS, NBC, Sirius XM "Dollars & Change", Huffington Post, Denver Woman Magazine (Cover Story), and is being profiled in the international project "200 Women"(Who will change the way you see the world). She also convenes global change-makers on topics such as leveraging the UN Sustainable Development Goals (SDGs), and helps build fundraising capacity for NGOs through a series of trainings held around the world.

An active supporter of the Women's Foundation of Colorado since 2007, Natalie is a former board trustee and has pledged $1 million to advance their mission of catalyzing community to advance and accelerate economic opportunities for Colorado women and their families. Her firm funds a Girls, Inc. scholarship entitled "Black Fox Scholars," rewarding high school girls for excellence in philanthropy. Her ultimate vision: *A world where men and women lead together with full opportunity and equality.*

Natalie is a member of Women Moving Millions; is an MCE Social Capital Guarantor; a delegate for the UN's Commission on the Status of Women; a delegate and contributor to the Skroll World Forum; a delegate and speaker at Opportunity Collaboration; and is on the Global Advisory Board of World Pulse.

Natalie is also an award-winning children's book author of the international SEL book: **"The Secret Adventures of Anonymouse"**. blackfoxphilanthropy.com

An Invitation

by Natalie Rekstad

*"If You Want to Go Fast, Go Alone.
If You Want To Go Far, Go Together." - African Proverb.*

My core belief is that the future hinges upon a more just and gender balanced world. As the beneficiary of the first and second wave of feminism, my mission is to help mobilize significant resources to bring about equality, on my watch and in my lifetime. It is a deep honor to be on this journey with so many awakened women and men who join me in this vision, all of us with unique roles to play.

Including you, Dear Reader.

Why does it matter? In the US alone, women continue to be more economically disadvantaged, experience much more violence, earn less, and are dramatically underrepresented in positions of leadership across all sectors.

But there's good news. As context, we're living in the most important time in the history of humanity. Never have we had so many viable solutions to suffering, poverty, and discrimination. Never have we had so many passionate people equipped to take direct action toward a thriving planet in which everyone can live with dignity.

We are living in the sweet spot of a world and time where women are more fiercely coming into their voice, thereby becoming more fully expressed and more fully empowered. In the US, women now have the economic chops to get equality over the finish line on a global scale.

Everyone is invited into this conversation and this movement, particularly men who are holding up the other **"Half the Sky"** (Kristof and WuDunn, 2008). In fact, I've noticed many fathers of daughters are some of the fiercest warriors of gender equity. These men encourage their daughters to take their full space in the world as the strong, spirited, dedicated leaders that they are capable of becoming.

It matters for our sons, too, who deserve to be raised in a culture that is free of the myth of superiority. In fact, it is their birthright to live fully expressed lives alongside our young women. To do so, they need to feel safe to be truly seen, heard, and valued as a whole, as well as to be encouraged toward great depths of thought and feeling. These are the men of tomorrow who will help bring about deep and lasting change.

We all benefit. Where there's more gender equality, there's more peace: Gender equality is a more reliable predictor of peace than a country's GDP or level of democracy. Advancing gender equality will add billions to the US economy. Gender diversity in leadership roles also boosts business performance. And close to home for all of us: Gender equality makes children's lives better. Teens in countries with higher levels of gender equality experience higher levels of satisfaction than teens in countries with lower levels of gender equality.

How do we get there Together?

Start Where You Are

No matter where you are or what you have to give, begin there. If you have time, give time. If you have a particular expertise, share it. If you can give emotional support, provide it. Most importantly, now more than ever, all men and women, either formally or informally have the ability to mentor a young girl or a young woman.

When I had only one time to give, I gave that time as a Big Sister. Over eight years I spent countless hours with Yvonne, my Little Sister. It was a profound experience for who I was and where I was in my life. Now in her thirties, she is a happy and thriving wife and mother of three.

With the time and treasure I now have, I am investing differently - more strategically toward lifting up an entire community or moving the needle on a core issue area. Yet it was the time with my "Little" (along with my own experience of growing up in poverty) that fueled my outrage and heartbreak as I watched Yvonne, her sister, and her single mother struggle with basic needs. This informs my strategic approach to philanthropy today, including founding Black Fox Philanthropy.

Our Deepest Passions Often Spring From Our Deepest Wounds

Like many of you, I am the beneficiary of the bold movement of feminism that exploded in the 1970s. Yet, at the time, I found it absolutely perplexing and in direct contradiction to the reality I experienced as a female in our culture. My ferocity and vision of women's empowerment stem from the wounds of a confused, frustrated girl whose wings felt clipped at an early age. But like so many women who care deeply about equality, I have transformed those wounds into a source of awakening and power.

If I could change one thing on this journey, it would be to change the view I had of myself as a victim of inequality as I strove to compete in a system set up for me to fail. Instead, I wish I'd shifted that view earlier, and adopted a **"Not On My Watch"** Warriorship and broken more barriers for myself and for the women who would follow me.

Pay it Forward

If your perspective is more anchored in gratitude, then "pay it forward." We stand on the shoulders of women who had the grit and drive to overcome unthinkable barriers. Perhaps you've been assisted by a country's education infrastructure, parents, mentors, and others. These gifts shepherd us toward a life that affords us the luxury of not only reading, but reading a book like the one in your hands. This basic right is denied to millions of girls around the globe.

Callings Call For Us To Grow Into Them

My strategic brain outperforms my wallet, so beyond my financial investments toward solving issues that are urgent and dear to me, to have far greater impact, I started a fundraising firm serving nonprofits called Black Fox Philanthropy.

Did I know all I needed to know when I began? No.

While I had the "right" professional background to begin the firm, I had to learn, grow, and learn and grow some more. I had my nose bloodied a fair amount but always strived to make things right, learning even more in the process. I love the imagery of falling flat on your face and after climbing to your feet, finding yourself a full body length ahead of where you were.

There are boundless rewards in taking the risk to respond to your calling. In my case, I'm deeply honored to work in a sector that labors toward eradicating global poverty, particularly because poverty lies beneath most of the world's suffering. I'm inspired weekly - sometimes daily - by the extraordinary visionaries and the missions we serve.

An Invitation

God has big plans for you in this movement toward equality, bigger than you may have for yourself. The world needs your complete voice at the table, in your relationships, and in the halls of power. I invite you to get in touch with your divinity and ferocity, to take your full space in the world as the powerful change maker of which you are capable.

To find your place in the movement and the world, take the first step - no matter how large or small. Your human potential is shaped and expanded as an instrument of service. Through the giving of your heart, time, talent, and advocacy for what you believe in, you'll rise to the challenge of your true calling. And in the response to that call, you'll find that deep happiness and purpose lies in playing your vital role among kindreds toward creating a more just and gender balanced world.

Welcome to the Tribe!

* * *

Natalie Rekstad
natalie@blackfox.global
www.blackfoxphilanthropy.com
www.anonymouse-aok.com

Melinda Gates

Co-Chair

BILL & MELINDA GATES FOUNDATION
Philanthropist, Business Woman, Mother
Passionate Advocate for Women and Girls

Melinda Gates

BIOGRAPHY

Philanthropist Melinda Gates dedicated her life to achieving transformational improvements in the health and prosperity of families, communities and societies.

"Bill and I started our foundation because we believe we have a real opportunity to help advance equality around the world, to help make sure that, no matter where a person is born, he or she has the chance to live a healthy, productive life."

Core to her work is empowering women and girls to help them realize their full potential.

"We know women and girls have a unique power to reshape societies. When you invest in a woman's health and empowerment, it has a ripple effect, helping families, communities, and countries achieve long-lasting benefits."

As Co-Chair of the Bill & Melinda Gates Foundation, Melinda shapes and approves strategies, reviews results, and sets the overall direction of the world's largest private foundation.

In 2015, Melinda created, **PIVOTAL VENTURES,** an investment and incubation company that enables her to bring together other new and emerging strands of her advocacy and philanthropic work focused in the United States.

Melinda received a bachelor's degree from Duke and an MBA from Duke's Fuqua School.

After joining Microsoft Corporation in 1987, Melinda helped develop many of the company's multimedia products.

In 1996, Melinda left Microsoft to focus on her philanthropic work and family.

Strong Women

Empower Other Women

by Melinda Gates

*"Women speaking up for themselves and for those around them
is the strongest force we have to change the world."*

I LOVE the idea of elevating women, because we're still trying to reach equality, but we aren't there yet. If we can show all these amazing things that women can do, it gives other women and girls role models to look up to and think, 'I could be like that entertainer -or lawyer-or entrepreneur -or mom who chooses to stay home'. It changes their aspirations of who they can be.

We all need (and need to be) role models.

I had some amazing teachers, like Mrs. Bauer in high school. She brought computers into the school when most schools didn't even know what they were. She was also raising three boys and getting her Ph.D. She was an amazing mom and gave me confidence in math and computer science.

Tell girls they can change the world.

If you're in tech, you're creating the future. We know girls lose their confidence in math in middle school, and that's the time they ought to be bolstered. Surround them with role models who will help them keep their confidence up. Only 18% of computer science graduates are women. We have to get more in tech.

No more warning her that Computer Science(CS) is hard. That it's all "brogrammers." That she just won't fit in. No more memos arguing that so-called biological differences make her less likely to be a good programmer. No more standing by as her dreams bump up against biases and barriers.

That girl deserves the chance to rise as high as her talents will take her. She deserves to have her voice heard, her perspective valued, and her great ideas funded. And the world deserves the chance to see what she can do. So how do we make that happen?

48

I think that if we want to see a sea change - if we want a wave of women in tech - then we need to open the flood gates. Right now, a lot of diversity efforts focus on getting more women into the so-called "pipeline." But that pipeline isn't producing much more than a trickle. And it has a lot of conditionals built in - a lot of if-then statements.

If you get girls to take the right math and computer science classes in high school, then they'll succeed in their intro CS classes in college. If they pass intro, then they will start their second-year courses on time and graduate in four years. And if they do that, then they can get their job in Silicon Valley.

Well, not every woman and girl is going to meet all those conditions. Many don't want to - and there's just no reason why they should have to in the first place.

So, in that spirit: what if we changed our basic assumption about how to diversify tech? What if we started from the premise that people get interested in computing at different times in their lives, in different ways, for different reasons? What if instead of one pipeline, we created new pathways - lots of them.

Or, to put it in coding terms: why not stop trying to get girls to meet the necessary conditions for each predetermined if - then statement? And why not start writing a series of for-loops?

Here are 4 for-loops we can use right now.

First: For girls growing up, let's create plenty of pathways to explore tech - inside and outside the classroom. Oakland high schools have a great model where they partner with companies. Students learn tech skills in class - and build projects with a mentor from the community.

Second: For women in college, let's make it clear that tech is a tool for solving real-world problems. That simple fact was a game-changer for a woman named Ellora Israni. She took her first CS class to fill a requirement. But then she realized, as she puts it, that "Computer science is as much about computers as chemistry is about beakers." When Ellora saw CS as a tool that could help her make the world a better place, she decided to major in it. Now, she's at Harvard Law, because she wants to use her tech skills to help improve our justice system.

Of course, not everyone finds their path into tech freshman year.

Third: For women already majoring in something else, let's offer programs that combine computing with the rest of their coursework - and lead to degrees in fields like bioinformatics.

Fourth: For women who discover their passion for tech at different times and different places, let's open more pathways into the field. For community college students, let's create bridge programs that lead to a bachelor's degree in CS - like they have at UC Davis. And for women who've already graduated, let's design master's programs to help them transition into computing - like they do at Northeastern University.

When you open up pathways like those, you make way for women like Christina Emerson. Christina grew up in a working-class family in Detroit. She always had a passion for computers - but she assumed you need a Stanford degree to make a career out of that. A community college showed her that just wasn't the case. And today, she has her own gaming company.

All of this comes down to the same point. For anyone and everyone who has talent and interest, there should be a way into tech. Not just one pipeline. Many pathways. That's how we'll turn the trickle into a torrent - and unleash a wave of talent. Many of you have already decided to be a part of the solution - a part of this wave.

Tackling the Imposter Syndrome.

Last fall, I met a computer science major named Patricia who shared a story about one of her first college exams. She'd studied and studied — and when her professor returned the test, he told her that she'd received the highest grade in the class. But Patricia said her initial reaction to this news wasn't pride or excitement - it was shock. She went as far as to suggest that the professor regrade the exam. She was so full of self-doubt that, even when presented with direct evidence of her abilities, her first instinct was to question it.

To a lot of you, this might sound familiar. If you've ever had a voice in your head telling you that everyone in the room must be smarter than you, that your success is due to luck instead of skill, or that the proper response to a compliment is a counter-argument, you've experienced the symptoms of impostor syndrome, too.

Impostor syndrome strikes all kinds of people, but evidence suggests it's especially prevalent among those who are under-represented in their fields - for example, women and minorities working in tech. When you're the only woman or person of color in the room, it can sometimes feel like you're in the wrong room.

As Proday Founder and CEO Sarah Kunst puts it, "There's a saying about succeeding in the face of systematic oppression - 'you have to be twice as good to get half as far.' Impostor syndrome says the opposite, that somehow you are half as good and got twice as far undeservedly."

It's frustrating to think about all the talented people who have worked so hard to rise so high - only to find that their deepest, darkest doubts have followed them there. Here are five suggestions for countering those negative whispers in your brain with something more empowering.

Recognize that even really successful people - experience this, too.

Ed Lazowska, the former chair of Computer Science and Engineering at University of Washington, says: "I feel like I'm an impostor, and the only thing that gives me confidence is that nobody has found me out in the past 40 years. So, the chance that I get discovered in the next couple of weeks is pretty low." If someone as credentialed as Ed has been feeling this way for decades, it makes sense that the rest of us will have our own moments of self-doubt, too.

Fake it 'til you make it.

When Dr. Sue Black, one of the UK's leading voices on technology, started teaching university level computer science, she was petrified. She didn't like public speaking, and she worried she wouldn't be a good teacher. She decided that to get herself through the experience, she would simply pretend to be someone else. Every time she stood in front of her class, she channeled a friend - a technology consultant who projected an enviable easy confidence. Soon enough, that confidence became a genuine part of who Sue was, too. She now says she hasn't felt impostor syndrome in years.

Use your time machine.

Psychologist and author Adam Grant says he manages his impostor syndrome with "the help of a wonderful time machine called my brain." Whenever he feels like he doesn't deserve to be giving big public talks, he thinks back to other times when he "wanted to run screaming off the stage" but ended up doing fine -which helps convince him that he'll be fine this time, too. Looking back on the past with the benefit of perspective helps him realize: "even if I fail, my future self will be glad I didn't fail to try."

Remember you can always improve.

I'll never forget what it was like to go into my first computer science class. The class was about processors, which I had never studied before, and also happened to be taught in a coding language I didn't know. What's more, the auditorium was full of men.

I thought: Maybe I shouldn't be here. Maybe I don't know enough. But when I realized that was the whole point: I was there to learn! I couldn't silence the voices in my head telling me "I'm not good enough," but I could amend them a little, to say "I'm not good enough-*yet.*" With that one change, that message stopped being devastating - and started being motivating

Question where these feelings are coming from.

Chances are, if you're a woman or a minority, you've received a lifetime of subtle messages telling you that you do not belong in certain fields. Maybe your brother learned more about computers while playing video games designed for boys. Maybe people were always suprised to see you were good at math. Maybe the men in your "weed-out" college courses had guys they knew in the department providing suggestions and reassurance, while you were flying solo. Realizing that the voices in your head are actually messages from a society that's set up in an unfair way can help you shut those voices down - and inspire you to prove them wrong.

Recently, I was struck by what Crisis Text Line Founder and CEO Nancy Lublin said when asked if she felt the imposter syndrome. Her answer was simple: No. She even added: "I work my ass off for everything I've achieved, and I remember that every day."

Let's commit to thinking more like Nancy. After all, it's easy to be your first worst critic. **What's harder - and far more important - is to be your own best champion.**

* * *

Melinda Gates
Co-Chair
Bill&MelindaGatesFoundation
www.GatesFoundation.org

Tina Tehranchian

Branch Manager, Senior Wealth Advisor
Assante Capital Management Ltd.

Tina Tehranchian

BIOGRAPHY

Tina Tehranchian, MA, CFP©, CLU©, CHFC©, is among the first-ever group of Certified Financial Planner(CFP®) professionals in Canada to receive the FELLOW of FPSC™ distinction from the Financial Planners Standards Council in 2011. This distinction formally recognizes individuals who helped advance FPSC's vision of seeing Canadians improve their lives by engaging in financial planning.

A financial advisor since 1991, Tina is a senior wealth advisor and branch manager at Assante Capital Management Ltd. and specializes in assisting business owners and self-employed professionals in building wealth and developing sound financial and estate plans. She also specializes in charitable tax planning strategies and helping philanthropic Canadians multiply their bequests to charities while reducing their taxes and leaving more money for their heirs.

Tina is often quoted as an expert in her field in the Globe and Mail, The Toronto Star, The National Post, and Metro, as well as in financial industry magazines. She has been featured in national radio and television shows such as BNN, CBC and CTV as a financial planning expert and is a frequent contributor at the Canadian Business Journal. She has taught personal financial planning at Centennial College's Center for Entrepreneurship for over ten years, and is the recipient of numerous academic, professional and community service awards.

Tina has been actively involved in her community and served as a director of the Markham Board of Trade and JVS of Greater Toronto, the treasurer of the Encyclopaedia Iranica Foundation, a founding member and first chair of the board of IC Network, a governor of Seneca College, a trustee of the McMichael Canadian Art Collection, a director of Mackenzie Health Foundation, Fort York Foundation, and Art Canada Institute, a member of the Research Campaign Cabinet of the Princess Margaret Cancer Foundation, and campaign cabinet for King Campus of Seneca College. She chaired the signature fundraiser for McMichael Canadian Art Collection, the McMichael Moonlight Gala, in 2012, 2013, 2016 and 2017, and co-founded and co-chaired the joy of Aging fundraiser for Mackenzie Health Foundation since 2009.

Love Abundantly, Give Abundantly Always Follow Your Passion

by Tina Tehranchian

"Be Clear About Your Values"

It is very important to have a clear idea of what your top values are in life. Your values will determine your priorities and your priorities will determine how you should live your life. If your lifestyle is not aligned with your values, you can never be truly happy and fulfilled.

Always Follow Your Passion

If you truly follow your passion you will succeed. You will live a happy and fulfilled life and will be able to maximize your contributions to your community, your family and to the world. Success is not all about money. There are many more dimensions to success and happiness than simply the financial dimension. The impact that you make on the life of your family, your community and the world is a big part of your success. If you measure succes only in monetary terms you will never be satisfied and will never feel truly happy. A life of following one's passion is a life well-lived and will likely be a life that is more impactful than a life spent in pursuit of financial goals only.

Be Compassionate

As a leader you need to be compassionate and need to deeply understand the needs and desires of the people that you are leading. Showing love and compassion for those who depend on you will ensure that you will be treated with love and compassion in your time of need.

Compete Against Yourself

The only person whose performance you need to beat is yourself. This will ensure that you will stay focused on your goals and will always strive to improve your performance without being distracted by having to compete with others. I always strive to improve myself in every aspect of my life and work. Humility is key. No matter how much other people think of your accomplishments, there is always room for improvement.

Care About Your Community

We all owe a great debt of gratitude to the communities that have supported us and have contributed to our success. This means that we need to ensure that we are giving back to our communities within our means. Give your time, talent and treasure and be confident that if you give you will receive. This is one of my core beliefs and I have lived my life following this principle. I think this is the only way we can ensure that we can make our world a better place. A world where everyone has this kind of mindset would be a truly great world to live in. We can each make our dent in the universe by giving back to our communities.

Always Put in Your Best Effort

No matter what project you are working on, whether it is self improvement, learning, volunteer effort, or a team project at work, make sure that you put in your best effort and give it your all. Every task you are involved in should represent your personal standards and your brand as an individual. Set the bar high both for yourself and for those around you. If you expect more of yourself, you will always try to do your best. If you want your team members to go beyond the call of duty and give each project their best effort, you need to do the same.

Lead by Example

Your team looks up to you and will follow your lead. If you are sloppy, they will treat that as a license to be sloppy too. If you strive for perfection, they will strive for perfection too. Remember that as a leader, you are the trend setter and the creator of the culture of your workplace. Set high standards and follow your standards so you can lead by example. The same principle applies to philanthropy. If you are raising funds for a cause, be the first to give and give the maximum you can afford. Your belief and conviction in the cause you are supporting and the financial support that you have given that cause, will compel those you ask for donations to follow your lead.

Seize the Opportunity

While many people believe in luck, I think seeking out and seizing opportunities is much more important than luck. Developing an ability to be nimble and be able to make a quick decision when good opportunities arise is key to success. Of course, seeking out opportunities, establishing connections, joining groups and putting yourself in environments that can lead to opportunities, are key to making sure that you will come across good opportunities. Your own enthusiasm and the time and effort that you put into seeking opportunities are a big determinant in finding them. Your decision-making abilities and nimbleness in recognizing good opportunities are crucial factors in being able to seize those opportunities. I think the biggest difference between leaders and followers is in their decision-making abilities. Leaders recognize good opportunities quickly, can make decisions under pressure and will often act swiftly once they have decided on the right course of action.

Give Abundantly

I strongly believe that you should give first to receive. I have been proven time and time again in my own life that this is true, which is why philanthropy has been and will be a major pillar of my life. The joy that comes from helping others can enrich your life. The donor receives much more from the donation in the form of greater happiness than the recipient of the donation. Find a cause that resonates with you and you are passionate about and support it to the best of your ability. Make a long-term commitment to a cause and get to know the organizations and charities that you support in depth. The more connection you feel to the cause that you are supporting the more fulfilling the experience will be for you. This can be one of the greatest sources of joy in your life and can make a big difference in the lives of others and your community.

Love Abundantly

For me the greatest value in life is love. Loving my family, loving my community, truly caring for my clients, my fellow human beings and future generations is the goal of my life. If I live my life in a way that I have loved abundantly and have put my time, money and talents to good use for my loved ones and for my community, I would consider my life a success.

* * *

Tina Tehranchian, MA, CFP©, CLU©, CHFC©
Assante Capital Management Ltd.
(905)707-5220
ttehranchian@assante.com
www.tinatehranchian.com

You cannot get through
a single day without
having an impact on
the world around
you.

-Jane Goodall

Mary T. Barra

GENERAL MOTORS COMPANY

Chairman and
Chief Executive Officer

Mary T. Barra

BIOGRAPHY

Mary T. Barra was elected Chairman of GM Board of Directors January 4, 2016, and CEO of of GM since January 15, 2014.

Prior to becoming CEO, she served as Executive VP, Global Product Development, Purchasing & Supply Chain since August 2013, and Senior VP, Global Product Development since February 2011. In these roles, Barra and her teams were responsible for design, engineering and quality of GM vehicle launches worldwide. Previously, she served as VP, Global Human Resources; VP, Global Manufacturing Engineering; Plant Manager, Detroit Hamtramck Assembly; and several other executive engineering staff and positions.

Barra's career in GM began in 1980 as a GM Institute (Kettering University) co-op student at Pontiac Motor Division. She graduated with a BS degree in electrical engineering in 1985, followed by an MBA from Stanford Graduate School of Business (GSB) in 1990.

Barra is a member of the Stanford University Board of Trustees and Stanford GSB Advisory Council. She also serves on the board of Directors of the Walt Disney Company, the Detroit Economic Club; and the Board of Trustees for Detroit Country Day School.

Mary Barra ranked #1 for the 3rd straight year on Fortune Magazine's List of the Most Powerful Women in Business. More details on her career can be found via Facebook, Linkedin and Twitter.

LEADERSHIP LESSONS
Tomorrow's STEM Leaders
by Mary T. Barra

"Do something you are passionate about, do something you love. If you are doing something you are passionate about, you are just naturally going to succeed."

Often I am asked if I'm proud to be the first female Chief Executive of a major automaker. On one hand, I'm proud to lead General Motors and the truly dedicated professionals who make great cars, trucks and crossovers for our customers. On the other hand, I'd like to normalize the oddity of a woman succeeding in a STEM -related field.

I never want to get a job because I'm female. I want to get it because I earned it and deserve it. Whether my hair is blue or purple, people should be judged on how well we do the job and deliver results the right way. That's how I like to be judged; most people are like that.

My very first job was at a grocery store, where I learned commitment to work. My father had an almost 40-year career at General Motors, and encouraged me to pursue STEM. I had a mother who believed *you could be anything you wanted to be in this country if you worked hard enough.*

My first job at General Motors was as a quality inspector on the assembly line. I was checking fits between hoods and fenders. I had a little scale and clipboard. At one point, I was probably examining 60 jobs an hour during an eight-hour shift. A job like that teaches you to value all the people who do a job like that.

Tomorrow's STEM Leaders.

What I learned as I got into this job - and it suprised me - a lot of people approached me and said: '*I see you in this role and because of your example my daughter is going to study engineering*- or *my daughter wants to be an engineer.*' I realized how very important for girls and women in our rapidly changing society to profit from the experience of role models they can look up to.

In fact, when I get the chance to chat with young girls, one of my favorite things to ask is what they want to do when they grow up. I've met some amazing students who are building robots, designing complex web applications and acing their science and math courses. One girl told me she wanted to create makeup - I told her, "*That's chemistry!*" Having a strong foundation in science and math allows you to approach whatever you want to do successfully.

Yet, I've also talked with girls who feel isolated in male-dominated classes, lack mentors, or are afraid to take risks for fear of failing. These girls need a path, they need support, they need more role models. All young girls start out believing they can do or be anything they want. Then, along the way, someone tells them that a career in technology requires a lot of math ... and they hesitate. Just like that, it's over. The dream vanishes and they choose not to pursue science, technology, engineering and math fields.

So today, we're intensifying our efforts to develop tomorrow's STEM leaders. Recently, we joined forces with **Girls Who Code,** and now we're expanding our scope by partnering with **Code.org, Black Girls Code, Institute of Play and Digital Promise**. Our partners and their programs bring unique approaches to reaching students at an early age - especially girls and under-representd minorities - to instill the skills and love of learning that will guide them through college and beyond.

I'm extremely proud of how many women we have in significant leadership roles at GM. I think there are more women in more senior roles than in 1980 when I started. You are rewarded a position of leadership by working really hard and earning people's respect who support you, and they're willing to extend a bit of their personal capital to say, 'Yes, I know so-and-so is going to do a great job in this new leadership role.'

In that light, let me share four leadership lessons from the speech I gave to the 2016 graduation class at my Alma Mater - Stanford Graduate School of Business.

Leaders Listen.

It's important to surround yourself with people who will challenge you and tell you when and why you are wrong. It's OK to admit what you don't know. It's OK to ask for help. And its more than OK to listen to the people you lead. In fact, it's essential. And, the need to listen doesn't diminish when you become general manager or CEO - *it increases.*

Leaders Care.

I was a student at Stanford in the late 1980s, when MBAs were frequently compared to Gordon Gekko, the character played by Michael Douglas in the 1987 film *Wall Street*. Gordon Gekko's mantra was simple: "Greed is good." Today, many people continue to view the business world with considerable disdain. Gallup's latest update on confidence in U.S. institutions reports that more than three-quarters of U.S. adults don't trust "big business."

As leaders in business, government, nonprofits, NGOs, or wherever your career takes you, you have a responsibility to help change the relationship and the reputation our institutions have with society. For me, at GM, that starts with customers. And no matter what business you go into, *you only win when your customer says you win.*

Leaders Inspire.

Your company's success depends on how well you satisfy your customers. When leading an organization, you must be concerned about the bottom line; but as a visionary leader, you think about more than just the next quarter. You think about the next decade, and your company's reputation and place in the world - even after 40 quarterly results.

More and more, today's employees want to be connected to a broader purpose. They want their companies and institutions to make the world a better place. I believe we can do both. I believe we are required to do both. I believe leaders set the tone, create the vision, and inspire behavior that allows organizations to best serve the needs of society.

At the end of the day, *all businesses are about putting people first* - because the only way to build genuinely successful businesses is through lasting relationships inside and outside the company. We do that by holding ourselves accountable, by doing what we say we are going to do, and by inspiring others to strive for some larger purpose other than just themselves.

Leaders Work Hard.

If you truly want to **"change the world,"** you need more than talent. Hard work beats talent if talent is not combined with hard work. Education opens doors. Talent open worlds. But hard work enables you to accomplish more than you ever dreamt possible.

I think about my mom and dad. My parents grew up during the Great Depression. My mom grew up on a farm in Northern Michigan. My dad grew up in an iron-mining area of upper Minnesota. They didn't have many advantages. They each had only high school degrees. But they believed in the American dream, and they worked hard to achieve it.

They taught my brother and me that there is no substitute for hard work and that work comes before play. They displayed the kind of passion and grit that allowed them not just to raise a family, but to build a foundation from which we could reach even higher.

The biggest message I can leave for young women is this: *don't start cutting off branches of your career tree unnecessarily early. Sometimes women say, I know I want to have a family or play in the local symphony, and they start pulling themselves out of their career path. You don't have to take yourself out of the running before you even start.*

Do every job you're in like you're going to do it for the rest of your life, and demonstrate ownership of it. That's when you'll get noticed. Work hard for what you want because it won't come to you without it. You have to be strong and resourceful and positive; knowing that you can do anything you put your mind to, and that perserverance is one of the most important secrets of success.

* * *

Mary Barra
Chairman & CEO
General Motors
www.gm.com

Dr. Natalie W. Geary, MD

Founder and Director
Private Pediatric Consulting, LLC

Dr. Natalie W. Geary, MD

Dr. Natalie Geary is the founder and director of Private Pediatric Consulting LLC. For over three decades, she has dedicated her career to the care of children and their families. Throughout her work, Dr. Geary has promoted health and well-being not only within her community, but also with under-served populations across the globe.

Dr. Geary's passion for cross-cultural work began when she worked at a leprosy hospital outside Delhi, India. Inspired by that experience, Dr. Geary received her bachelor's degree at Harvard University, concentrating in Medical Anthropology, and her medical degree from Johns Hopkins. After completing her residency at NYU/Bellevue Hospital Center, Dr. Geary practiced pediatrics in New York before moving to New Mexico where she founded a non-profit, Mobile Pediatrics, to provide medical care to children across the state. Dr. Geary also worked to establish programs in Indonesia, Thailand, and Malawi focused on nutrition and health maintenance for children and pregnant women.

In 2009, Dr. Geary accepted a position as Director of Executive Medicine at the University of Miami School of Medicine, and became the hospital's Director of International Health and Chief Patient Experience Officer. After more than five years of senior hospital management, she resigned and returned to primary care, to prioritize more active one-on-one patient engagement, and time with her family.

Dr. Geary is also an author and speaker, and has received many awards recognizing her work. She was elected, among other awards, Pediatrician of the year 2017, Humanitarian of the Year 2018 and Empowered Woman 2018. Dr Geary also founded vedaPURE, a simply natural, honestly pure skincare line, which she was inspired to create after years treating children and nursing mothers who experienced negative side-effects from steroid creams.

Dr. Geary attributes her success to being blessed by her own children, who taught her the most about what is important in life, to long hours of research, and to her commitment to bettering the lives of children and their families.

OUR CHILDREN ...OUR FUTURE

by Natalie W. Geary, MD

"The purpose of life is to live it, to taste experience to the utmost, to reach out eagerly and without fear for newer and richer experience" - Eleanor Roosevelt

I am very lucky to have been lovingly raised by committed parents, blessed by an extraordinary education, and supported by three wonderful daughters and a family that I not only treasure but also rely on. My life has been a journey that I feel grateful for. Despite my extensive training and experience, I credit my time raising three daughters as the most important work of all.

My philosophy and approach to my work originated when I went to India as a young woman. While working at a leprosy hospital outside of Delhi, India, I was inspired by the resilience of the people I met who were facing impossible challenges but found many different ways to cope.

At seventeen years old, I returned from India determined to find a way to contribute, even in small and individualized ways, to help change the future of children and their families. I witnessed the effort, the love, and the struggle for many people trying to give their children more than they had been given.

When I arrived at college, I was intent on using the opportunity to study these challenges and experiences from a more academic perspective. I concentrated in Medical Anthropology, a field that was just beginning to grow at that time. The field examines and analyzes how culture and society impact healthcare processes, individual healthcare beliefs, and health-seeking behavior. My thesis analyzed health care beliefs and utilization practices in cancer patients, comparing patients at Sloan Kettering Cancer Center in Manhattan and Tata Cancer Center in Bombay(Mumbai).

After college, I went to Johns Hopkins for medical school. I believe that medical school does, and should, teach prospective doctors how vulnerable people can be, especially when they are sick, or a family member is suffering. It also taught me that every day means something, but it can be hard to stay in the moment, focused on the well-being of the patient, not the lab tests and treatments being ordered.

Raising my children helped me to stay in the moment, to remem--ber the true risks and fears felt by my patients and their families, and the value of every day. Being a parent, working hard to provide the best for your family, is hard work. I learned more from my parents and my children than I did from any textbook I had to memorize in school.

I have tried to bring these important lessons with me throughout my career. While living in New Mexico, one of the poorest states in the country, I started a non-profit to provide medical care to communities that were often inaccessible and suspicious of those they saw as outsiders, including doctors. Mobile pediatrics dispatched doctors, myself included, to schools and other public locations to screen children for developmental delays and underlying diseases.

My staff and I provided vaccines, eye tests, screening tests, and overall assessments free of charge to the children and their families, I treasured the experience of getting to know the children and their families, gaining their trust, and empowering them to make the best choices for their health and well-being.

At other points in my career, I have engaged in similar work around the world. I re-member being in Jojokarta, Indonesia, going to an impoverished village, and meeting a young woman with what I diagnosed as an abdominal tumor. My non-profit, Mobile Pediatrics, had funds to support her care. Long after I had returned to the States, she wrote me, updating me on her health and well-being. I wept with joy.

"The mystery of human existence lies not in just staying alive, but in finding something to live for."
- Fyodor Dostoyevsky, The Brothers Karamazov

Giving is critical. Getting feedback from the giving is a gift. We all have ways to give, whether it's through financial contributions, spiritual support, or skilled labor on behalf of others, people make fun of me for believing that the glass must always be looked at as half full, that life is to be looked at through rose colored glasses. However, the experiences I have had only reinforced that belief.

Throughout my career, I have spent many years studying Ayurvedic medicine and philosophy, drawn from ancient Indian texts and practices. I have been drawn to it since I first learned about it at age 17 while working at a leprosy hospital outside of Delhi, India. My later thesis research essentially aimed to understand how Indian cancer patients faced death and dying without such anger, remorse and bitterness compared to their counterparts at a large cancer hospital in New York.

What I learned from them was that these patients accepted the varied reasons - spiritual, dietary, behavioral, and other life events - that contributed to why they were ill. They were then able to utilize a variety of sources of care without feeling that any one or two were in contradiction with the casuality of disease. They embraced the many opportunities to find well-being even as they accepted their diagnosis.

I have always been inspired by this approach to health, well-being, and care. I have dedicated my career to sharing that message - that people should try to embrace many ways of thinking and coping and healing - with families. Nowhere is this approach more important than in the care of children.

We all share in the project of raising and shaping the next generation. We must take that responsibility seriously, while recognizing the inherent gift of it all. For my future, I will continue my quest to empower others to raise their children to be happy and healthy, hoping to make small but significant differences in peoples' lives around the world.

* * *

Dr. Natalie W. Geary, MD
www.integrativeHealthByDrGeary.com
786.375.1515
www.vedaPURE.net

Love ♥ Children

I heard you tell the children at play
They shouldn't laugh and scream,
The looks you give, the words you say,
Can step on a child's dream.

I saw the look of disdain, clearly in your eyes,
Wouldn't you rather hear joy - than pain -
In the children's cries?

They were shaking rain from their shoes one day,
When your husband passed their way,
And all that he could think to say is:
"What a dumb thing to do!"
Doesn't that bother you?

It bothers me, it gives me a chill -
A chance remark can cripple or kill.
On behalf of the children - *hold your tongue -*
Has it been that long since you were young?

Didn't you ever play in the rain?
Or trace your name on a window pane?
Or scream with joy while playing a game?

Never wound a child's pride,
Or hurt a child's mind,
Even when you scold or chide -
You can still be kind.

In the future generation
Lies the destiny of our nation -
So love our children
Treat them as you would your own.

And If you must correct them . . .
Kindly - *watch your tone!*

© Pat Sampson

Catherine Gruener

Psychotherapist/Parent Trainer
Owner/Creator of Encouragement Parenting
Division of Gruener Consulting, LLC

Catherine Gruener

BIOGRAPHY

Catherine Gruener is a psychotherapist who works with parents and parents of neuro-atypical children, helping them understand their strengths and transform their weaknesses to help them and their children thrive, creating healthier and stronger communities. She is an advocate for gifted and profoundly gifted children, known internationally for her work with gifted children and families, and as author of *'Parenting Young Gifted Children: What to expect When You Have the Unexpected'.*

As a licensed clinical professional counselor and national certified counselor certified in Positive Discipline, with a Master's degree in Neuropsychology, second Master's degree in Clinical Counseling, and two decades' of highly influential work in the mental health field, Catherine has impacted other's mental health and wellbeing through her research, international community mental health work, government and community mental health organizations, national and local parent organizations, and currently through her counseling practice and Encouragement Parent trainings.

Though she enjoys the therapy relationships in her clinical work, she loves teaching and speaking to parents, from private gifted schools like Quest Academy, national organizations like the Davidson Institute, to larger audiences from around the world like at the Best You Expo Long Beach. Encouragement Parenting is an enlightening and empowering approach that uses intuitive, expressive, and experiential trainings to help parents help themselves and their children, find and fulfill their purpose, and live their best lives.

Catherine is passionate about sharing her knowledge and has been recognized for outstanding leadership by the international association of TopProfessionals (NY), Elite American Educators, Elite Women Worldwide, Marquis Who's Who, "TopFemale Executive", and as a "Top 101 Industry Expert" in parent education.

She strongly believes that through mutual respect, encouragement, empowerment, and using our gifts to contribute to the larger community, people gain dignity and self-worth-conditions essential for healthy communities.

The Winding Path to Self-Actualization

by Catherine Gruener

"The real gift we can give to the world is being our authentic selves."

We Disintegrate to Rebuild

I wasn't especially close with my best friend's younger brother. Like most high school kids, we didn't pay much attention to our elementary school siblings. He was a good kid, I guess, I didn't think much about it.

And then it happened. Even I could spot the change after that car hit him. His personality, demeanor, and temperament changed drastically. And my best friends' life was upended.

My friend's brother suffered a severe traumatic brain injury, and I watched my friend's family fall apart. Her brother's personality changed, his temperament changed, and I began to question how much of him was still 'him'? This question haunted me and drove me to get a degree in psychology and a master's degree in neuropsychology. This random, awful accident fueled my fascination with the mind and body connection, and my pursuit to understand the 'soul'.

There were ample opportunities to study brains in the Neuropsychology master's program in Colorado, and at my first job at a rehabilitation center. I pushed hard to distinguish the real source of disorders. I knew that people were more than an "organic brain syndrome." This was where I got involved in being a voice of others ... trying to advocate for more holistic mental health.

In 1996, I found myself married and living on Saipan. Saipan of the Commonwealth of the Northern Mariana Islands(CNMI) is an island in the Pacific Ocean within the Ring of Fire. It is hot, humid and attracts Asian tourists with its luxury hotels. Of more than 300,000 people that live along the Northern Mariana Islands, I was one of only a few white, blonde-haired American women. I stood out as a Howlie (not local) who did not know the local customs or speak the local language.

Catherine Gruener

Even for an introvert who savored time alone, I started to feel isolated, and when my position was finally approved by the government, I poured myself into my work as a therapist, mental health assessor, and community counselor. I lived on boxed and canned food and bathed in brackish water. I avoided wild dogs and feral cats on the village streets, and WWII undetonated bombs, cannons and guns in the jungle. I survived Super Typhoons, a seven-point earthquake, a tsunami threat and a divorce, and the work was challenging as well. I took a rather large knife away from a hysterical client and talked another down from using a gun on himself in the lobby.

This culture, so different from the Western culture I'd grown up within, generated a completely different way of speaking, sharing, politicking, and relating to others. The mainlanders are communal, holistic and matriarchal. They trust intuition more than deductive reasoning, respect established hierarchies, barter fervently but avoid confrontations. As a lead on a CNMI mental health statistics team I negotiated research agreements with U.S counterparts in Washington, I became awestruck by the differences the Eastern and Western cultures brought to the negotiating table.

Everything I knew, believed, and imaginated fell away. As a therapist, I watched myself go through this, and studied how pervasive our cultural norms are on identity, and strictly our environment frames our view of life. I discovered how desperately we need connection with others and what true connection is. I saw how much humanity has in common and how diverse our thinking can be. I suffered through the process and power of healing and reconnected with my soul.

At home in Chicago, I enrolled in a master's degree in Professional Clinical Counselling at Adler University. Adler's theory resonated with my experiences at home and abroad and started to answer my big questions about Soul.

Lessons Learned.

Being has far less to do with Id, Ego, survival and self-interest than it does our experience as an intact soul growing up in a social environment.

We come into this world intact. We have everything we need– our life path, our life purpose, all of our strengths — to lead a healthy, fulfilled, meaningful life.

As we grow up we learn, from our parents (first), how to function in the world. We're learning how to eat, how to walk, how to speak a language ...but that is not US. We are MORE.

The real process of self-actualization is our journey towards who we really came into this world to be. It's all about blending 'from within' and 'from outside,' and continually revealing the soul.

You, right now, are a complex algorithm of the soul you were born with, and every interaction you've had with your surrounding world.

The strongest impressions we take away from interactions are about *how we belong and how we are significant.*

When we believe that we don't belong, that we're not important, that we are, in some way, less than...we'll try out a range of behaviors to make ourselves whole again. But in doing so, we can move equally away from our true selves.

I see it all the time.

Children try out behaviors and find belonging in misguided ways. Like children who feel they matter only when they're in charge - which results in all kinds of power struggles with their parents. Children who act out, get noticed, and connect attention-getting behavior with feeling seen. Children who don't realize they're hurting and lash out in revenge with the simplest expression they know:" I hate you." Or the child whose feelings of inadequacy overwhelms them until they simply give up and withdraw.

Extreme behaviors work *too* hard for belonging and significance. They are *over-compensatory.* Sometimes they 'kind of' work - they ease our immediate psychological distress. But they don't work forever, and they don't actually land us any closer to our true Essence or Being.

Encouragement Parenting addresses our own over-compensatory behaviours, those patterns that turn up in our parenting, those lessons we learned as we reacted to interactions we had when we were children. We heal the past, so we can focus on understanding the child. It then gives us the tools to create connection, so our children listen and respond positively and our relationships with them and ourselves improve

Catherine Gruener

Supporting Our Children.

Here is how you can help your children stay connected to their essence.

Recognize that every child comes in with their own temperament and their own being. Honor that child for who they are. It helps to understand that we're always shaping their sense of belonging and importance in the world. When you're confronted with disruptive behaviors, you know that you're bumping up against pain and misunderstanding.

Approach with curiosity and wonder. Ask a child questions rather than telling them what they feel or try to fix their problem. When you predict what they're going to say or do, you impose your idea of who they are onto them; you're not truly seeing them for who they really are and can be.

Connect, Teach and Problem Solve. Connect before you correct or teach. We connect by understanding that children are doing the best that they can. They are attempting to get their needs met with behaviors that may be useful, or not so useful. Your child wants to do well, they want to find belonging and significance in their world, and they sometimes can do it in not so useful ways. Teach your children how to take their gifts and share them with the world. Support children learning how to solve their own problems.

We need you, and your kids, and everyone on the planet, to share their gifts with the rest of the world.

* * *

Catherine Gruener
(872)216-5860
catherine.gruener@gruenerconsulting.com
www.encouragementparenting.com

Virginia 'Ginni' Rometty

CEO and President
IBM CORPORATION

Virginia 'Ginni' Rometty

BIOGRAPHY

Virginia 'Ginni' Rometty, CEO and President of IBM, the first woman to head the computer technology giant, is an inspiration to women the world over. She began her career with IBM in 1981 in Detroit and worked her way up the hierarchy with her amazing marketing skills and never-say-die attitude.

In 1975, Ginni won a scholarship to Northwestern University, and earned a degree in Computer Science and Electrical Engineering from Robert R. McCormick School of Engineering and Applied Sciences. After graduation in 1979, she joined General Motors Institute. In 1981 she joined IBM Detroit as a Systems Engineer, and her impressive performance did not go unnoticed. In 1991, she became part of the IBM Consulting Group.

In 2002, Ginni led the successful integration of Price Waterhouse Coopers Consulting, winning her many accolades. This acquisition was the largest in professional services history, creating a global team of more than 100,000 business consultants and services experts. In 2009, she was promoted to Senior Vice President and Group Executive for Marketing, Sales and Strategy. She propelled company growth by venturing into business analytics and cloud computing, playing a major role in the production of 'Watson', the Jeopardy! winning super-computer.

In 2011, Ginny became IBMs first female CEO and President. The following year she was appointed Chairperson when Samuel Palmisano stepped down. Ginni serves on the Council of Foreign Relations; the Board of Trustees of Northwestern University, the Board of Overseers and Board of Managers of Memorial Sloan-Kettering Cancer Center, and as a member of the Latin America Conservation Council.

In 2014, Ginny was featured in the PBS documentary, The Boomer List. She was honored with Honorary Doctoral degrees from Northwestern University and Rensselaer Polytechnic Institute.

Fortune 500 named her to its List of the 50 Most Powerful Women in Business for 10 consecutive years, and she topped the ranking as #1 in 2012, 2013 and 2014. Forbes named her to its 2014 List of the World's 100 Most Powerful People. In 2015 Fortune Magazine selected Ginni #3 of the Most Powerful Women of the World.

THINK

IBM's long-standing mantra
by Virginia 'Ginni' Rometty

> *"I think of myself not as a woman CEO of IBM,*
> *I think of myself as a steward of a great institution."*

What has always made IBM a fascinating and compelling place for me is the passion of the company, and its people, to apply technology and scientific thinking to major societal issues. Planes don't fly, trains don't run, banks don't operate without much of what IBM does.

You're never going to fully embrace your career unless what's behind it is something you love doing. Ever since I was a kid I was smitten with math and science. I'm the kid that tried to take Latin in school because I felt if I could understand the root of everything, then I could understand why it worked. That was what took me into engineering. And it's the reason I stayed. Engineering teaches you to think critically and solve problems.

Every day I get to 'Think' and work on everything from digitizing electric grids so they can accommodate renewable energy and enable mass adoption of electric cars, helping major cities reduce congestion and pollution, to developing new micro-finance programs that help tiny businesses get started in markets such as Brazil, India, Africa.

I am BIG on encouraging everybody to be a critical thinker, and to focus on lessons learned in every situation. As I always say to our own team - something didn't work out? What are the lessons learned?

Let me share three stories that illustrates a few lessons I learned that have served me well.

Never let anyone define you -- only you define who you are.

I grew up in a middle-class family in suburban Chicago. It was a simple, but happy childhood. I'm the oldest – I have a brother and two sisters. Like many, we went to Sears once a year for our school clothes. I remember one -- just one family vacation—a camping trip.

Virginia 'Ginni' Rometty

My father left my mother—in fact, he left us all. My mother had never worked a day in her life outside our home—and in a very short time she found herself with 4 children, soon no money, no home, no education. What would she do?

My mother was determined to never let anyone define her as victim -- or worse—a failure. As fast as she could she set out to make it all OK for us. She found a way to go to school during the day to earn a college degree—while working at night—so we could quickly make it on our own. By watching her, I learned that no problem couldn't be solved, that 'actions speak louder than words'. To this day, I think about that in everything I do.

Growth and Comfort Never Really Co-Exist.

The recommendation I make when I'm mentoring folks is – take a risk. Ask yourself, when have you learned the most? I guarantee it's when you took a risk. It's the times when you're most challenged that you're truly growing career-wise. So, if you're feeling anxious as you start a new job, that's a good sign, you're learning. This has been a really important realization throughout my own career.

During mid-career, my comfort zone was challenged. The executive I worked for – he was my mentor - was moving to a new position. He announced with great excitement that I would be offered the job as his replacement. My reaction? Instead of feeling elated, I felt uneasy. "It's too early... I might not be ready...I'll be ready in a few more years..." I needed to go home and think about it.

That evening, my husband—now of 36 years—listened patiently and said: "Do you think a man would have answered that way? I know you. In six months, you will be telling me you learned everything you need to know and are ready for the next challenge..." He was right. I accepted the offer.

Work on Something You're Passionate About -- That's Bigger Than Yourself.

My husband and I were at a theater in NYC in September 2012 when someone called my name. It was the CEO of a healthcare company. He was so enthusiastic about "Watson", (named after Thomas J. Watson, IBM's founder) he could barely contain himself. "We will change the face

Virginia 'Ginni' Rometty

of healthcare", he exclaimed! 'Watson', is a question-answering computer system to help providers and health care organizations manage population health, deliver more efficient care, engage patients and consumers, and optimize business performance – through the power of data-driven insights.

Artificial intelligence is one of 50 things that Watson does. I'm especially proud that IBM chose one of the toughest areas – healthcare. IBM's moonshot, is to have Watson help beat cancer. It is being taught by the very best doctors in the world, from Cleveland Clinic to the Memorial-Sloan Kettering and many others. We are now able to bring improved cancer diagnoses to thousands of patients today, and through our network of hospital partners we have extended the same care to remote places that seldom see an oncologist — from rural parts of the U.S. to villages in India.

It's hard to think of a bigger goal. And that's the type of thing that keeps me energized, and makes me proud to be an 'IBMer'.

Let's celebrate female pioneers in computing

Why the history lesson? Because the past is prologue. And the fact is that women played a vital role in driving all areas of computing: tabulating, programmable—and now, cognitive.

How many have heard of Ada Lovelace?

Ada Lovelace has been called the world's first computer programmer.   In the 1840's Ada worked with Charles Babbage on his 'Analytical Engine' considered one of the world's first computers. Ada wrote essentially what we'd today call an algorithm for Babbage's machine. In her notes, Ada described how codes could be created for the device to handle letters and symbols along with numbers. She also theorized a method for the engine to repeat a series of instructions, a process known as looping that computer programs use today. Ada also offered up other forward-thinking concepts in the article. While Charles Babbage is known as the 'Father of Computers', Ada Lovelace is not popularly known as the "Mother of Software," even though she should be.

Naval Officer Grace Hopper

Fast forward to World War II. Women were enlisted in the war effort to help develop technologies against the Axis powers. Perhaps the most colorful among them was Naval Officer Grace Hopper who worked on an IBM computer named Mark I.   Also known affectionately as "Amazing

Grace," Hopper pioneered the first compiler for a computer language program—a predecessor of COBOL and later programming languages that would make modern computing possible. In Walter Isaacson's 2014 book, "The Innovators," he wrote that Grace Hopper's boss, Howard Aiken, initially balked at having a woman on his team. Over time, however, Aiken recognized Grace's skill and talent and promoted her to be his primary assistant and programmer. During her lifetime, Hopper was awarded 40 honorary degrees from universities across the world. A college at Yale University was renamed in her honor. In 1991, she received the National Medal of Technology. On November 22, 2016, she was posthumously awarded the Presidential Medal of Freedom by President Barack Obama.

Katherine Johnson, Dorothy Vaughan, Mary Jackson

Fast forward to the 1960s. How many know the inspiring story of these three brilliant African-American mathematicians at NASA— who were the key brains behind the launch of John Glenn's Project Mercury orbit around the Earth, as well as Apollo 11's flight to the moon, that galvanized the world. I am so delighted that these geniuses finally receive the credit they deserve in the 20th Century Fox film —"Hidden Figures"—the film was nominated in 2017 for three Academy Awards including Best Picture.

Success is no accident. It is hard work, perseverance, learning, studying, sacrifice and most of all, love of what you are doing or learning to do. The best advice I can give to young women is to focus on math and engineering -- as they provide the foundation to teach you to think critically and solve problems – and no matter what profession you choose that will be a skill that will serve you well.

One day we're going to look back, and whatever this era will get called, it's going to put a premium on math and science. All the women before you have paved the way for the greater things you will do. I wish you the best as you continue defining the future.

* * *

*Virginia "Ginni" Rometty, CEO
IBM President and Chairman
www.IBM.com*

FAMOUS QUOTES
by Women We Love and Admire

- *A lot of people say 'sexy' is about the body. But to me, 'sexy' is a woman with confidence. I admire women who have very little fear. Allegra Versace*

- *And the day came when the risk to remain tight in a bud was more painful than the risk it took to blossom. Anaïs Nin*

- *Vision without execution is hallucination. Arianna Huffington*

- *Have you ever seen innovation where someone didn't take a risk? Jean Case*

- *To feel valued, to know, even if only once in a while, that you can do a job well is an absolutely marvelous feeling. Barbara Walters*

- *Nobody on this earth has the right to tell anyone that their love for another human being is morally wrong. Barbra Streisand*

- *Cherish forever what makes you unique, cuz you're really a yawn if it goes. Bette Midler*

- *Power's not given to you. You have to take it. Beyoncé*

- *No one changes the world who isn't obsessed. Billie Jean King*

- *You can't give up! If you give up, you're like everybody else. Chris Evert*

- *A girl should be two things: classy and fabulous. Coco Chanel*

- *Find out who you are and be that person. That's what your soul was put on this Earth to be. Find that truth, live that truth, and everything else will come. Ellen DeGeneres*

- *I have an appetite for life. I'm in love with beauty and things and people and love and being in love, and those things I think, on the inside, show on the outside. Gloria Vanderbilt*

- *The trick in life is learning how to deal with it. Helen Mirren*

- *Take criticism seriously, but not personally. If there is truth or merit in the criticism, try to learn from it. Otherwise, let it roll right off you. Hillary Clinton*

- *The challenge is not to be perfect...it's to be whole. Jane Fonda*

- *Don't compromise yourself. You are all you've got. Janis Joplin*

- *To do what you wanna do, to leave a mark - in a way you think is important and lasting - that's a life well-lived. Laurene Powell Jobs*

- *I used to be Snow White, but I drifted. Mae West*

- *The minute you settle for less than you deserve, you get even less than you settled for. Maureen Dowd*

- *Do all the good you can, by all the means available, in all the ways you can,in all the places you can, all the times you can, for as long as ever you can. Mia Farrow*

- *One of the lessons that I grew up with was to always stay true to yourself and never let what somebody says distract you from your goals. Michelle Obama*

- *Knowing your value means owning your success. Owning your success means acknowledging your achievements. By acknowledging your achievements you build confidence. Mika Brzezinski*

- *Women are leaders everywhere you look - from the CEO who runs a Fortune 500 company to the housewife who raises her children and heads her household. Our country was built by strong women and we will continue to break down walls and defy stereotypes. Nancy Pelosi*

- *That is your legacy on this Earth when you leave this earth: how many hearts you touched. Patti Davis*

- *Any time women come together with a collective intention, it's a powerful thing, magic happens. Phylicia Rashad*

- *If you're someone people count on, particularly in difficult moments, that's a sign of a life lived honorably. Rachel Maddow*

- *You have to be courageous in all that you do. You have to know when there's a time to fight. Sonia Sotomayor*

- *You can't be that kid standing at the top of the waterslide, overthinking it. You have to go down the chute. Tina Fey*

- *Remember, each one of us has the power to change the world. Just start thinking peace, and the message will spread quicker than you think. Yoko Ono*

Marjorie Saulson

President, Vibrant Vocal Power
Public Speaking and Messaging Coach

Marjorie Saulson

BIOGRAPHY

Named both Top Public Speaking Coach of the Year and Top Motivational Speaker of the Year by the International Association of Top Professionals, Marjorie Saulson is the *Show Up, Speak Up, Stand Out, and Succeed* specialist.

She empowers her clients to uncover their unique and authentic messages, develop powerful presentation skills, and overcome their fear of public speaking; so that they can share their gifts with the world, and reach their income and professional goals.

A magna cum laude graduate of the University of Michigan, with a BA in Liberal Arts and a Teaching Certificate; an MA in Audio-Visual Education, and a tireless life-long learner; Marjorie brings extensive training and experience to her work with her clients.

During her career as a professional volunteer, she served as a certified adult trainer, a magazine editor, chair of a multitude of events including two symphony designer showhouses; and as president of numerous organizations, including the Detroit Symphony Orchestra Volunteer Council, the Association of Major Symphony Orchestra Volunteers, her synagogue Sisterhood, and regional and international positions for Women's League for Conservative Judaism and the United Synagogue of Conservative Judaism.

She attributes her success, both in her volunteer and her business careers, to her passion for helping people realize the fullness of their potential, and her determination to continue expanding her own skills to further enhance the service she offers both to her clients and to those who take advantage of the excellent materials she provides in her online courses, on her website, in her blog, and in her videos.

A recipient of many honors, Marjorie is a native Detroiter (aka a Motor-town/ Motown girl), and enjoys living in Metro Detroit with her husband Saul, and within a mile of her children and her grandchildren. (She considers herself one very lucky lady!!)

MASTERING PUBLIC SPEAKING

Why Is Effective Communication So Important?

by Marjorie Saulson

"There are two types of speakers: those who are nervous and those who are liars." Mark Twain

Clichés become clichés because they point to an acknowledged truth (at least as it is understood and believed by people in the current culture).

It has now become an acknowledged cliché that people prefer to do business with people they know, like, and trust; in other words, with people with whom they have created a valued relationship.

Yet how do you create a relationship with a stranger, or with someone with whom you would like to work, or to serve through your business?

The answer is to be able to communicate effectively with that person--to have conversations, ask questions, listen attentively, and to provide relevant and well-timed information-all of which leads me to share how I define public speaking.

My Oddball Definition of Public Speaking

When people think or talk about public speaking, what generally comes to mind is giving a speech. It just so happens that this definition of public speaking is usually at the top of the list of what people fear the most; even ahead of death, disease, and divorce.

Yet I define public speaking differently. I define public speaking as any time you speak to someone other than yourself.

Think about it! Do you feel comfortable at networking events? How about online, creating a video or audio recording? What about leading a workshop?

How willing are you to pick up the phone to make a request of someone, or to speak to a potential client, or to ask someone for a donation if you're raising funds for a worthy cause?

Do you feel confident and effective when you are having a sales conversation with a potential customer or client? Are you able to build that all-important *know, like and trust* factor that leads to sales and/or referrals, and an on-going positive relationship?

Do you speak up for yourself if someone takes credit for your idea, your suggestion, your work? If you work for someone else, how eager are you to ask for a raise or a promotion? Can you handle a question to which you don't know the answer without jeopardizing your authority status?

When a family member, friend, or aquaintance asks an intrusive question, are you able to set the boundary around your privacy without creating ill-will or starting a feud?

If you answered no to any of the above questions, there are generally two reasons why:

1. You haven't yet learned the skills necessary for this particular activity.
2. You are afraid to open up your mouth and speak up, even if you have learned the skills.

What Causes Such Fear of Public Speaking?

Intellectually many of us try to convince ourselves that it's silly to be afraid of giving a speech, or speaking up on various other occasions. After all, there is no physical danger in doing so - no tiger to jump out and bite us as we speak, no lightning bolt to come out of the heavens and down through the ceiling to strike us down.

So if there's no physical danger, what's the problem? The problem is that while we may feel physically safe, we don't feel emotionally safe from what I call the unholy trinity of public speaking fears - criticism, rejection, and failure.

These fears represent the unhealed wounds of our childhood, wounds we suffered when we were too young to have the resources to heal them. Any time we feel them as adults, it's a reminder that we have some healing work left to do. In the meanwhile, here are some suggestions for handling these fears.

The Fear of Criticism

Criticism often seems to be the go-to strategy for turning us from unruly children into civilized adults. So it's no surprise that we can get emotionally upset when someone criticizes us. Here are a couple of strategies for you to consider. To apply these effectively, it's important to come into your adult self as much as possible.

- Consider the source. Do you respect the person criticizing you, or is this a person who regularly snipes at other people? If you don't respect this person, then maybe what he or she says isn't worthy of your respect either.
- Unless you believe that you know absolutely everything there is to know about the topic under discussion, ask yourself if there might be some germ of an idea or suggestion that is worth considering. Sometimes good ideas and suggestions can come badly dressed in unfortunate language.

The Fear of Rejection

Eliminate the illusion that what you have to offer is a good fit for everyone to whom you offer it. Whenever you share an idea, a suggestion, or an offer with someone, view it as a sorting mechanism. Here are the 5 possible results none of which is a judgement on your personal worth as a human being.

1. Your offer is a good fit for that person right now.
2. It will be a good fit at some later time.
3. It's not a good fit for that person.
4. That person might refer you to someone for whom it's a good fit.
5. You get no response at all from that person.

Always remember: whatever the current result, you have planted the seed of a future possibility.

The Fear of Failure

It took Thomas Edison several thousand attempts until he found the right material for the filament to create the first functional light bulb. When asked why he kept working on this invention when he had failed so many times; his answer was that he hadn't failed, he had just eliminated a bunch of things that didn't work.

You don't pick up a tennis racket and expect to play center court at Wimbledon after a lesson or two.

When something doesn't work out right away; instead of asking what went wrong, it is much more helpful (and much less discouraging) to ask yourself these two questions:

1. What went right that can be retained in the next iteration?
2. What pieces of the process need to be improved?

This approach will move you along the road to doing it better the next time, and the next time after that, until you eventually move on to success.

The 3-Legged Stool of Effective Communication

Just as a 3-legged stool requires all 3 legs in order to fulfill its function successfully, there are three crucial aspects to any effective communication. I call them the *What*, the *How*, and the *Allow*.

WHAT IS YOUR MESSAGE?

- Is the topic relevant and of interest to the people in your audience?
- Does it cover (and perhaps solve) a problem that is important to them?
- Are you sharing a solution and the benefits of your solution?
- Is your message well-organized around an outline that allows people to easily follow your line of thinking?

HOW ARE YOU PRESENTING IT?

- If you are giving a speech, are you speaking clearly and loudly enough so that people can hear you easily (or using a microphone correctly)?

94

- Are you using appropriate gestures to emphasize the meaning of your message?
- Are you varying the tone of your voice so that you don't put people to sleep by standing there and droning on and on? (This is especially likely if you are reading your speech without adequate training on how to do it well.)
- Are you actually looking at the people to whom you are speaking?
- If you are writing something, can people actually read it easily?

DO YOU ALLOW YOURSELF TO SPEAK?

- Do you use effective strategies to overcome your fear of speaking in public?
- Do you know strategies for handling the usual last minute nervousness before you speak?

Why It's So Crucial For You to Speak Up

- You create positive relationships with family, friends, and people with whom you wish to do business.
- You serve those who may desperately need what you have to offer.
- You feel good about yourself and proud of what you are able to accomplish.
- You fulfill your personal and business goals.
- You grow into your full potential as a human being.
- You do your part to make this world a better place.

MARJORIE'S MOTTOS

- Misers make good ancestors.
- It is better to be a *has been* than a *never was*.
- Nothing improves your vision like company coming.
- My jewelry is insured. Please keep my calendar safe.
- If you don't schedule it, chances are it won't get done.
- A professional volunteer is someone who gets aggravated for free.
- Houses, gardens, and businesses are always in a state of becoming.

- There is no failure as long as you learn the lesson it has to teach you.
- When you stay inside your comfort zone for too long, it starts to feel like a jail.
- In life there is no stasis. You are either shrinking or growing. Choose to grow.

Quotes from Other Sources

"There is no limit to what you can accomplish, as long as you don't don't mind who gets the credit." (From a sign in the office of a dear friend.)

"Changing the toilet paper roll does not cause brain damage." (From a sign I bought for one of my bathrooms.)

"Do one thing every day that scares you." Eleanor Roosevelt

"Stay away from negative people. They have a problem for every solution." Albert Einstein.

"The person born with a talent they are meant to use will find their greatest happiness in using it." Johann Wolfgang von Goethe

More from Marjorie

Visit my website: *https://www.vibrantvocalpower.com/* to find:

- My complimentary report, **Overcome Your Public Speaking Fears.**
- More information in articles on my blog page, and in videos on my media page.
- Descriptions of my programs and private coaching opportunities.
- Testimonials from people with whom I've worked.
- Links to my social media sites.

* * *

Marjorie Saulson
President, Vibrant Vocal Power
info@vibrantvocalpower.com
Google Phone:: 248-716-1516

Renee Villanova

International Event Planner
CEO Global Wonderlust, LLC

Renee Villanova

BIOGRAPHY

The oldest of two children, reared by a single mother with little more than strength and determination, Renee remains the first person in her family to earn a college degree. Her studies focused on Humanities, yet she earned her degree in Liberal Arts.

As a Private/Corporate Flight Attendant, early career opportunities included visiting every continent, except Antarctica. This afforded her quality time with passengers, many familiar names and faces, sharing of their lives and offering their wordly perspectives. She was honored to be a part of a medically necessarily, International trip extending the life of a woman with alternative treatment.

Some of the most memorable periods of that time were the times she spent with Christopher Reeve, who quickly became one of her personal heroes. She deeply admired the close relationship he had with his young family, his determination to advance medical research, and his positive attitude during what would have been dark times for most after his paralyzing accident on horseback. Once during an inflight mechanical situation, his positivity became a source of comfort to her, the rest of the crew, as well as his family and medical team onboard. He truly was a super man!

The next overlapping chapter of Renee's career is where she discovered professional passion. Planning, managing, and overseeing group travel and events offers more unique experiences than she would have ever imagined. Rarely does one have such exciting challenges as renting NASCAR tracks with cars and drivers or entire private islands. She was *'over the moon'* to spend time with American Patriots Buzz Aldren and Neil Armstrong on separate occasions. From sitting in Green rooms with former US Presidents, Comedians, Musicians, Actors and Politicians to swimming with Manta Rays in Hawaiian seas to driving into giant schools of migrating Sardines in Mexico, her 'work' might be bucket-lists to some. She welcomes these adventures and for that reason loves her 'work' life.

Foster Healthy Communities

by Renee Villanova

*"What you do makes a difference, and you have to decide
what kind of difference you want to make."*
~ Jane Goodall

Having traveled all over the US and to over 40 countries, I've learned first-hand how much communities differ. We each establish 'communities' in various areas of our lives. Our professional community may differ greatly from our social or neighborly community, yet their importance to our life directly correlates to the roles we play in them. One of my goals is to **positively contribute** to each of my communities.

Travelers have the privilege of temporary membership in many communities, some dependent on revenues brought by tourism. **It is crucial to have a social consciousness** when traveling. At Global Wonderlust, we do exactly that. Our events incorporate Community Service Activities and source local suppliers and organizations often positioning our budgets as mutual beneficiaries. Travelers appreciate the thought put into local, often handmade treasures they are gifted. We often organize hands-on events, leaving a wake of gifts, food, toys, bikes or other useful items behind. Partnering with local organizations for the local placement of these items helps serve their communities. These efforts introduce travelers to local causes emphasizing their impact. While on location we prioritize limiting waste, recycling and buying sustainable. We limit single use items, favoring washable or compostable dishware/flatware to disposable. We **remain cognizant of the environmental sensitivities and humanitarian concerns** in every destination.

Live your values

In 2015, I invested my first rental property, a beach house in Puerto Rico, having no idea what this community had in store for me. A few years later Hurricane Maria put my sourcing and organizational skills to the test. I had to help! **Failure was NOT an option** I immediately took to social media to organize donation drives for emergency rescue items, necessities, clothing and food for victims. **Generosity and compassion prevailed.** The bigger challenge was the logistics arranging transport for items gathered in my home in Grapevine, Texas. Another motivating success! All items were delivered in volunteers' suitcases, mailed via USPS directly to needy homes, flown as cargo on commercial flights (free) or on luxury private jets (donated). Our donations were placed directly in the hands of those in need, many times expedited to their doorsteps avoiding the red tape so many organizations faced. With the help of an online booking tool, I had an opportunity to provide housing accomodations to hard working volunteers. These people left their safe, comfortable communities, mostly on the mainland, to aid and care for those in need. For the next four months, volunteers and recovery teams rotated through my house (with no or limited water and power) working tirelessly on rescue and recovery efforts. Together they rebuilt homes, delivered life-saving supplies and rescued pets and lifestock, while I helped with fund raising and gathering essential donations. Many of those amazing people remain on the island, while others are now working in other areas of need. Many volunteers established tremendous bonds through shared compassion.

Surround yourself with good people doing good things

In December of 2017, I left my home in Texas to join those in Puerto Rico to assist a hands-on, door-to-door neighborhood assessment effort. Our teams entered neighborhoods in need to help determine how better the private sector could support families. We brought solar lights, small cash donations, baked goods and some holiday cheer to families living without power and in many cases, very limited resources. This effort was coupled with a private, nationally supported Toy Drive for children in Rincon, a mountainous western coastal town. It was a successful, combined effort pioneered by one generous local man and orchestrated by teams of islanders and mainlanders. Neighbors and strangers working together and delivering relief and toys - some not even speaking the same language. I will always remember the faces of the families we touched, the warmth we were greeted with by those going through so much. I entered these projects hoping to make a positive change for others, having no idea the positive change they would make in me.

I quickly learned **jumping in headfirst is great way to sharpen your skills.** The successes of the post-Maria recovery efforts motivated me to increase my involvement. Supporting the nutritionally insecure,

100

the environment, veterans, first responders and various other causes are now part of my life's routine. Through my business, we often include an opportunity to do something special for a cause important to the group's affiliations. We challenge ourselves to stay creative and deliver uniquely fulfilling experiences, often using small opportunities to educate and connect. **People are the most important part** of every event. Great consideration is given to those attending as well as those impacted by our travel footprints.

Foster Healthy Communities

Many of us have a desire to do more; no excuses - **find a way to make your mark!** Surround yourself with **good people doing good things.** I am fortunate. I meet amazing people doing fantastic work all over the world. I try to follow their lead and **live by example.**

Where you can start -

- **Check with local foodbanks, animal shelters or retirement homes, many welcome volunteers.**
- **Booking travel? Ask your hotel about their initiatives, they often have opportunities for guest involvement.**
- **Plan family activities with enlightening moments. Help educate future generations to care enough about their communities to contribute**

We all have a responsibility to contribute to the wellbeing of our diverse communities. *The efforts put forward today make for a better tomorrow.*

* * *

Renee Villanova
Global Wonderlust, LLC
leadership@globalwonderlust.com

Marie-Flore
Lindor-Latortue, Ph.D

Educator
Radio/TV Host
Professional Business Consultant

Marie-Flore Lindor-Latortue, Ph.D.

BIOGRAPHY

Dr. Marie Flore Lindor-Latortue ("Dr. Flore") is the founder of the Association of Exchange and Development of Activities and Partnerships (AEDAP), a non-profit organization recognized in the State of Florida since 2007. Following in her father's footsteps, AEDAP offers a platform for various organizations that gather every year for a leadership retreat.

A capacity building consultant, Dr. Flore is a motivational speaker and educator. The first woman of Haitian descent to serve in the Florida Commission on the Status of Women, she helped identify women who made a difference at the national level between 2004 and 2008; she also led the Commission's Public Relations Committee.

Proponent of the "Gade Tèt Ou" philosophy, Dr. Flore believes one's success is made possible through constant practice on self-questioning and self-awareness. Dr. Flore, a keynote speaker at business events, university functions, and professional convocations, shares her leadership skills with attendees of different backgrounds. Dr. Flore is a radio host with 23 years of experience; her culturally sensitive programming making a difference in lives of many minority groups in Miami Dade County. October 2011, she blended radio and television, creating Radio/Tv with Dr. Flore, the first trilingual programming of its kind. The 58-minute broadcast attracts listeners and viewers in North Miami and beyond, is fast growing and is taking social media by storm.

Dr. Flore, recipient of many honors and awards, published many articles on leadership and public health. A seasoned public speaker, she's been educating Florida residents about Health Services Administration, General Education, and Leadership for the past 19 years.

She and her husband Roland Latortue are the proud parents of Raphael and Lucphillipe Latortue.

IMMIGRANTS MATTER

The Soul of America

by Marie-Flore Lindor-Latortue, Ph.D.

> *"Give me your tired, your poor, your huddled masses,*
> *yearning to breathe free,*
> *The wretched refuse of your teeming shore, Send these,*
> *the homeless, Tempest-tost to me,*
> *I lift my lamp beside the golden door. "*
>
> ***Emma Lazarus***

God has blessed America and what it stands for - a land of diversity - a melting pot. People from all over the world come to its shores as immigrants in search of a better life for themselves and their families. Now, more than ever, ALL of us need to understand that a great country is built by a genuine love for ALL people and the powerful desire to make a difference.

Born in Haiti, I grew up with a deep appreciation of all America represents. I am proud of the love and respect of my country's immigrants, the soldiers who fought, and all who contribute to this country in every way and every day. I am in awe of the immigrants including myself and my family, and our endless struggle for a better life, overcoming the obvious limitations and boundaries of our environment, we are dedicated to the values and inspiration of the promise expressed by the Statue of Liberty. Yes, I cry when I see what is happening to all we hold dear. Like children separated from their families and the story of a 39 year old landscaper, Jorge Garcia, father of two and spouse of a U.S citizen, having known no other country than the US for 30 years, deported back to Mexico. Today, Alejandra Juares, wife of an Iraq Veteran, and mother of two young daughters, ripped from her family after 20 years and deported back to Mexico. The shame of it all.

104

"Gade Tèt Ou" - is the philosophy I share with the world. These three words in Kreyòl, my native language, are powerful. They mean: "Watch out." or look at yourself. In this context, its meaning is to conduct self-assessment, cultivate self-awareness, and use the inner-power of introspection that helps define us as human beings, from birth to our passing. Gade Tèt Ou is an ongoing self-questioning practice that empowers us in all areas of life, including education, health, finances, and relationships.

We honor that spirit by allowing it to shine onto the lives of people to help them make that first step toward their own greatness. The combination of so many varied backgrounds, all seeking the unification of a better way of life is an inspiration and example for all to see and follow, even in these turbulent times. Identity is the foundation of all societies. The Haitians who chose the United States as a safe haven to overcome the traumatic experience post the earthquake of 2010, may well be deported back to a land where they have no home and no families, forced to seek a new identity.

We want to read and hear from our leaders. Whether entrepreneurs, artists, speakers, veterans, and teachers, whether poor or wealthy, we must lead with empathy. We must acknowledge the suffering of those yearning to be free. Even if you are not an immigrant yourself, surely you have met, or heard of exceptional stories of the tenacity and triumph of individual immigrants and groups that powerfully speak of today's immigrants as the builders of this country too, through education and faith, hard work and service in the army, leadership and wisdom, and participation in politics.

105

We are ALL born equal in the eyes of God. Ultimately, we live, we learn, and we evolve in the way we treat one another. Freedom is our guidance and power source. We, as Americans must bring back kindness; we must be the shining light that America represents. Like all families, our children carry our dreams and hope for the future. And yet to witness families being torn apart is wrenching. Our youth must be shown compassion and hope to forge their future based on freedom to reach their God given potential. We all know that to preserve the future of the country is to insure the well-being of our youth; and show through love and example that their opportunities are limitless.

Gade Tèt Ou, Watch Out, means creating connections in order to spread a universal message: women and men in a position of leadership have the power to turn a life around, while giving this and future generations a greater opportunity to make a difference without prejudice based on race, social status, education, wealth, and privilege. This ultimately is the meaning of the inscription on Lady Liberty that serves as a constant source of inspiration to immigrants arriving in these United States and to people seeking freedom from around the world.

* * *

Marie-Flore Lindor-Latortue
PO Box 565853
Miami, Florida 33256
florelatortue@gmail.com
www.florelindorlatortue.com

The Story of the Statue of Liberty
Liberty Enlightening the World

The French Sculptor Frédéric Auguste Bartholdi, renowned for his grandscale designs, watched the exquisite richness of the changing colors of sunset outline the Notre Dame Cathedral, and dreamed that one day he himself would create a monument of everlasting significance. *"When I find a subject grand enough, I will honor it by building the tallest statue in the world, one whose beauty and majesty will inspire the ages."*

As he shared his vision with the renowned scholar Edouard de Laboulaye, the latter suggested Bartholdi travel to the United States to make the first contacts toward a joint project to commemorate liberty, convinced that such a project would be undertaken by the common efforts of the two nations. *"There will always be a bond between the United States and France"*, Laboulaye said, adding, *"When hearts have once beaten together something always remains, among nations as well as individuals."*

Supercharged with the energy of great dreams, Bartholdi sailed to America. *"I saw the New World in a pearly radiance."* As he entered New York Harbor, he envisioned a grandiose monument rising above the city's skyline. It was to be a tall and proud woman, of classic beauty and modern spirit, her arm raised as a beacon of freedom. He named her *"Liberty Enlightening the World"* as he rapturously sketched his vision. A vision so powerful and catalytic that for the next fifteen years, from conception to inauguration, hundreds of thousands of American and French men and women from all walks of life would be swept up in the financing, construction, and enjoyment of the creation of the mighty symbol of liberty.

Bartholdi extended his love for his mother from his soul to his creation: she was the model for the classic beauty of Liberty's face.

Each milestone toward the statue's completion was a major news headline, a cause for mass celebration. Early in 1884, the head of Liberty rose above the rooftops of Paris, ready for her journey to the New World. When Liberty arrived packed in dozens of huge crates, she had to await funding for a pedestal to stand upon.

"Let's not wait for the millionaires to give this money," editorialized Joseph Pulitzer from his newspaper, *The New York World*, called *'the people's paper,'* as he urged Americans to contribute funds for the Pedestal. ***"This statue is not a gift from the millionaires of France to the millionaires of America, but a gift from the whole people of France to the whole people of America."*** Thousands responded, many of them school children. When the pedestal was near completion, the mortar for the last block was sprinkled with pennies, nickels, and dimes, honoring the givers of love.

On July 4, 1884, *"Liberty Enlightening the World"* was lifted onto her pedestal with great fanfare and formally presented by the people of France to the people of the United States.

Throughout his lifetime, many honors were bestowed upon Frédéric Auguste Bartholdi for his great achievements. None of the honors, not the most effusive accolade, however, would faintly compare to the rapture he felt as he sailed from New York Harbor contemplating the silhouette of his beloved creation against the entrance of the Golden Door of Freedom for all peoples. ***"Goodbye, my daughter, Liberty. I am glad you are home at last,"*** he whispered into the wind.

For over a century, *"Liberty Enlightening the World"*, has majestically stood through the storms of winter and the scalding of summer, shining the light of love upon the sons and daughters of liberty, pristine symbol of the enlightened consciousness shared by freedom lovers everywhere.

Cordelia Gaffar

Founder, Workout Around My Day
Author & Speaker, Mom of Six

Cordelia Gaffar

BIOGRAPHY

Cordelia Gaffar, Founder of **Workout Around My Day**, is unique in many ways. Her high level of skill and sincere empathy is the driving force that enables her to become a recognized leader, a sought-after speaker, and effective motivator for women seeking to live a more balanced life.

Cordelia, author of three inspirational books, co-author of a fourth, her personal experiences are at the heart of her teachings. She sought medical attention for postpartum depression after the birth of her second child, which led to habits resulting in extreme weight gain.

Determined to make positive changes in her life she began a serious study of nutrition, exercise, and a positive mindset. In less than one year lost over 60 pounds, and became nourished and energized in mind, body, and spirit.

Giving birth to four more children during her spirited entrepreneurial journey, it became crystal clear that most women need additional tools and support to cope with the demands of motherhood while pursuing a career.

Cordelia, a certified Essentrics Instructor, incorporated her love of dance, and the 'superpower' practices responsible for the dramatic shift in her own health and well being into a 90 minute Body Soul work-out group sessions for women to express and release 'emotional baggage' in a safe and nurturing environment.

After a spiritual retreat to Bali, she created a workshop that incorporates physical and emotional tools resulting in "**The Body Soul Shift**". group coaching programs, to meet you where you are and attract the people and circumstances that ultimately propel you to share your personal gifts with the world.

Cordelia Gaffar

FINDING YOURSELF
The Body Soul Shift

by Cordelia Gaffar

*"Life prepares us for blessings through opportunities
to better understand gratitude."*

To find ourselves, we must continue to grow emotionally, physically and spiritually. The time you grow most is after facing and overcoming a problem or challenge. We must never allow ourselves to think and say **"Why did this happen to me?"** Instead if you focus on the solution you will have the opportunity to grow to a new level of understanding, knowledge and ability to grow stronger, able to do more than you ever dreamt possible. When you face a challenge, ask yourself: **"what can I learn from this?"** Each one of us creates our experiences by the thoughts we think and the words we speak and the beliefs we hold.

I found myself by facing my own need for self-healing. Two years into my entrepreneurship journey of self-development and evolution, it re-awakened my grief for my father. He passed away over 20 years before. He had a successful private law practice, owned property, and before retiring, became a highly respected judge. He was my mentor and my friend. In my moment of personal crisis, I needed his kind, loving presence. I felt lost.

My emotions occupied my very being and held me captive for a long while. Finally, I came to terms with the fact that nothing would change unless I did. I resolved to change things. I began by studying the symptoms of unresolved grief. I had them all -- the curved posture, the rounded shoulders, the slouched back. The heaviness of sadness sends alerts throughout the body to protect itself. That's when inflammation takes root in the fat cells and the lymphatic system. Crying continually activates the adrenal system - not in a beneficial way. It's not long before you have a ripe environment for all systems down.

The solution involved deep breathing, movement, nourishment, embracing my feelings, practicing gratitude and experiencing true sensuality. I spent most of the past 21 years feeling half of my emotions, nourishing half of my mind and soul, practicing half gratitude. So how could I feel everything and truly find myself able to love and live with gratitude for my many blessings? Little by little over a period of time, I developed a method that allowed me to become fully present and experience the full range of my emotions and feelings. I used my passion to illicit compassion for myself and others. I got out of my head and into my heart and body!

The Body Soul Shift.

Start by tuning into your body with movement. For me it is dance. For others I work with its yoga, running and breathing. Whatever you choose, move all of you-your shoulders, core, hips, thighs and feet. This is where we store old patterns, habits and negative energy. Be gentle and notice any places of resistance, tension or pain. Make notes in your journal or log. Feelings originate in the heart and emotions in the mind. Self-sabotage happens in the mind. Accept that you choose your vibration or emotions based on feelings in your heart. Recognize what you see may be colored by your emotions. Where and how are you in this moment? This is your present reality.

Sweet Talk.

Sweet Talk will help you transcend the fight and experience a flight into the realm of higher consciousness. Tuning into your body daily will change the way you experience your emotions. The connection with body and emotions creates a beautiful language that emerges from your heart. **Sweet Talk.** When you place yourself in the hands of a beautiful principle in which you appreciate who you are - faith in yourself strengthens.

Remember, it is your opinion that is most important; it doesn't matter what anyone else thinks. You must learn to ask yourself empowering questions every day. If you look for and focus on the good, you will feel good. If you focus on the negative you will feel sad and depressed and not have the motivation to do all the great things of which you are capable. One way to set up a new pattern of thought is to ask yourself every morning: **"what's good about my life?"** and **"what am I excited about today?"**

Radiate and shine.

You must realize that you deserve to feel great every day. It can't be a wish or a "should be," it has to be a **must,** Think and radiate your inner feelings to the outer world. **"I am committed to doing what is necessary to feel happiness, respect, love and satisfaction every day."** This kind of thinking activates the law of attraction and pulls your desires to you. **Enjoy yourself.** You are totally in control of how you feel on a daily basis. Affirm: **"My thoughts attract everything I want and need. People are positively affected by my presence. I can't wait for new experiences. I truly feel that I can do anything. Everything is constantly in flow."**

Go with the flow & embrace abundance.

Flow is where your **Body Soul Shift** happens. I took luck out of the equation and walked into my ultimate purpose. The need for meaning and purpose is the greatest single drive in human nature. The final piece is embracing abundance. Imagine for a minute, every emotion unsuppressed, and being yourself unfiltered in a state of abundance. Glorious!

Taking a step further, radiate what you want and witness your deepest desires fulfilled. Aim for the stars. Believe that success comes easy for you. Say, **'I enjoy sharing my gift with the world.'** Discover your ultimate gift and embrace it. **Being different is not a problem, it's a blessing.**

Respect your body. It is your temple. Commit to nourishing your body with sleep, wholesome food and movement. Take an honest inventory of your closest companions. Do they nourish your life and fuel your purpose?

Finally to be totally fulfilled, you must have a sense that you are making a genuine contribution to society. This is possible for each of us, whether we contribute by being a giving, loving person, or by inventing something of value to humankind.

Before countries can break bread together, neighbors must. The belief in being able to fulfill our own dreams also includes the inspiration of countless others who follow their own path to greatness. When you genuinely love and accept yourself for who you are -- you grant the same freedom of expression to others. It includes love of family, a clear purpose, and priorities that guide us and keep us moving forward with hope for the future to claim all that life has to offer.

* * *

Cordelia Gaffar
cordeliagaffar.com
cordelia@workoutaroundmyday.com
304-268-2803

JENNY XU

TOP 1% PRODUCER USA
RE/MAX MASTERS REALTY

Jenny Xu

BIOGRAPHY

Jenny Xu began her career in the real estate field more than 25 years ago. She has consistently been ranked the #1 agent in her office and region and has been in the top 1% as a top producer in RE/MAX U.S. for many years. She has been the recipient of numerous awards, too many to list, such as the Circle of Legends, Lifetime Achievement, and Diamond Awards.

Jenny takes pride in understanding her clients. In fact, one of her past clients stated "Jenny is an incredibly intelligent realtor, who advises us along the way, meanwhile listening to our goals."

Her vast experience allows her to effortlessly find the right home for her clients. Jenny excels in her communication skills, and exhibits superb leadership skills, needed to guide her team successfully and efficiently.

Jenny is also an expert making speedy, expeditious homes sales for her clients while obtaining top dollar in the negotiation process. One of her former clients said this about Jenny "We have bought and sold 6 properties using various realtors and our experience with Jenny has far exceeded all others. She more than fulfilled everything she said she could. Jenny sold our house for more than other houses up for sale in our neighborhood and she sold it within two weeks of the listing".

Most of Jenny's new clients come by way of referral. She has over 50,000 clients in her database and many refer their friends or relatives to Jenny. As a result, Jenny is in very high demand throughout many communities in Southern California. This is a reflection of her long-standing past performance as well as from creating trust and confidence with her clientele.

Beyond the above, Jenny possesses a very pleasant, easy-going personality that makes each client feel at ease through each real estate transaction. Her goal is to make sure the home buying or selling process is not only enjoyable, but also, a memorable experience.

How I became Successful

"If You work with passion then you will enjoy what you are doing."

by Jenny Xu

My story is an improbable one. I moved here from China several decades ago. I could neither read nor speak English. I first lived in Texas and where I lived there were hardly any Chinese people. One of the first problems I encountered was that I was accustomed to eating Chinese food, yet the only Chinese restaurant I could find was Panda Express; a far cry from real Chinese food. The only American food I could stomach were French fries, which I ate every single day for a month. It seems quite funny now.

I subsequently moved to California where I decided to make my home. I love California especially the weather, the convenience and the diversity of ethnic groups and cultures. These early years in China and the USA have shaped my philosophy of life and of the Real Estate profession:

Each real estate agent faces a great deal of demands in his or her chosen career path. I am sure every agent wants to be successful and a top producer.

Here are some Key points to success:

- Delivering quality service and being honest with all clients and endeavors.
- Placing priority and focus on the needs of the consumer/client.
- Becoming an expert in the real estate market by dedicating as much time as necessary to study all facets of it.
- Understating how marketing works. Advertisement via the internet is not sufficient. A successful realtor identifies a multiplicity of marketing sources, including, but not limited to newspapers, magazines, and flyers.
- Creating opportunities for team-building with your staff so that morale is always positive. If your staff feels good about themselves they will perform much better than if their morale is low.

117

- Identifying best practices in marketing. Do not cut corners or economize on advertisement approaches. For example, advertisement flyers in color will yield far better results than in black and white.

Success in the real estate profession is suprisingly pretty straightforward:

- You need to always strive to be the best that you can be.
- Always put your best effort in everything you do.
- Always work hard and be willing to go above the call of duty.
- Always be available to your clients.
- Be like a "proton" and always stay positive.
- Place a priority focus on your clients' needs.
- Be willing to be a teacher as well as a student, and never stop learning.
- Adopt the attitude that "failure is not an option".
- Always think big, the opportunities are limitless and the sky is the limit.
- Do not be afraid to take risks or big steps if that is what the job requires.
- Stay 100% committed to what you are doing, avoid distractions.

In conclusion, there are no instant successes or magic pills to success in real estate. I believe each one of you can become successful but it will require patience and commitment.

I can honestly say I love my career. Yet, the best part is not the commission or awards that I earn; rather, it is the appreciation I receive from my clients and the satisfaction I derive by seeing the happy expressions on my client's faces when I help them sell their homes or find the homes of their dreams. That really warms my heart.

* * *

Jenny Xu
(626)674-7368
jenny@jennyxuhome.com
www.jennyxuhome.com

Dawn C. Sequeira, Esq.

Immigration Attorney
Legacy Immigration, LLC

Dawn C. Sequeira, Esq.

BIOGRAPHY

Dawn C. Sequeira is the Owner and Principal Attorney of Legacy Immigration, LLC., a full-service immigration law firm that focuses on complex immigration.

A native of Orange County, California, Dawn C. Sequeira attended undergraduate school at American University where she received her Bachelor of Science Degree in 2001, with a major in Biology and minor in Criminal Justice. Dawn attended law school at American University, Washington College of Law in Washington, D.C. where she obtained her Juris Doctor in only 2½ years.

Dawn has successfully represented individuals and corporations before U.S. Citizenship and Immigration Services, The Administrative Appeals Office, the U.S. Department of State, the Executive Office for Immigration Review, and the Board of Immigration Appeals. In 2015, Dawn opened Legacy Immigration.

With over 10 years of experience contributing to legal initiatives on behalf of small business, Fortune 500 companies, hospitals and the federal government, Dawn has a reputation for being a lawyer who goes the distance to get the best possible outcome for clients by delivering "winning immigration strategies."

Dawn became passionate about cancer research after her grandmother passed away from uterine cancer. She became a lifetime member of the American Association of Indian Scientists in Cancer Research (AAISCR) and established the organization's first scholarship program in 2017.

Dawn is a patron of the performing arts, primarily the Baryshnikov Arts Center in New York City, NY. In an effort to support domestic violence victims, Dawn is a financial sponsor for ASHA for women (a non-profit serving domestic violence victims from South Asia). Dawn is also passionate about other social issues related to veterans and animal cruelty.

Dawn is admitted to the New York Bar (2008), the District of Columbia Bar (2009), and the U.S. Supreme Court (2016).

Love One Another

by Dawn C. Sequeira, Esq.

> *"Just as I have loved you, you also should love one another."*
> *(John 13:34)*

Although I am relatively young, I do not take my mortality for granted: here today, gone tomorrow. But once I'm gone, I think to myself: "What will people say about me at my funeral? Will they say that I was kind to strangers? That I gave freely of my time and resources to help those in need?" I want to be remembered as someone who loved unconditionally.

There are many ways to define "success." I measure success by the societal impact I had in making this world a better place. I do my best to be a good person, to embody charitability, compassion, honesty, kindness, mercy, forgiveness, patience (and patience certainly is a virtue). I want to know that during my time on this earth, I made a difference in at least one person's life, and if I'm lucky, I made a difference in many people's lives.

We are all equal. There is no caste system. There is neither rich nor poor, black nor white, no lesbian/ gay/ bisexual/ transgender/ questioning/ queer/ intersex/ asexual/ ally / two-spirit, Hindu/ Christian/ Muslim/ Atheist/ Agnostic/ Buddhist/ Mormon/ Jewish, Democrat/ Libertarian/ Republican/ Conservative/ Independent. We all came from dust and to dust we shall return. There is no escaping it, so while we are on this earth, we should be the best people we can be.

There is enough hatred in our world. We all have a choice to choose love over hate, unity over discord, forgiveness over vengeance, mercy over cruelty. Don't think, "I'm only one person. What I do doesn't matter.

If each one of us does our best to show love to everyone we meet, we could transform this world. Do your part to love one another and leave vengeance for God; *"an eye for an eye makes the whole world blind."* - Mahatma Gandhi

Dawn C. Sequeira, Esq.

Like all of those who came before me, including my parents, I have a chance to make my mark in this great country. The legacy I choose to leave behind is to help as many foreign nationals achieve their American Dream so they can make this country a better place for future generations.

Before I incorporated my law firm, I had to think of a name. I knew that I wanted my practice to focus exclusively on *immigration* law and that I didn't want to name the firm after myself because I wanted a name that the firm could "grow into." More important, though, I wanted a name that would outlive me, yet continue to propagate my vision. I wanted my firm to be my *legacy*. So with that, I named my firm "Legacy Immigration."

In terms of my firm's vision, I reflected upon the history of this great country. Why did intending immigrants flock to Ellis Island? Because it afforded them the opportunity to attain their American Dream: a better standard of living for themselves or their families, an opportunity to obtain an education or provide a better education for their children, a safe place to practice their religion, or flee from persecution.

In 1931, James Truslow Adams wrote a book entitled, *The Epic of America,* in which he defined the American dream as *"that dream of a land in which life should be better and richer and fuller for everyone, with opportunity for each according to ability or achievement. It is a difficult dream for the European upper classes to interpret adequately, and too many of us ourselves have grown weary and mistrustful of it. It is not a dream of motor cars and high wages merely, but a dream of social order in which each man and each woman shall be able to attain to the fullest stature of which they are innately capable, and be recognized by many others for what they are, regardless of the fortuitous circumstances of birth or position."* (p.214-215)

I wanted my motto to remind foreign nationals of what the American Dream is, a national ethos of the United States, with the ideals of: democracy, rights, liberty, opportunity and equality.

In my mind and heart, the United States will always be known as the land of opportunity and freedom. I wanted my law firm to preserve this legacy; with that, my motto was born: *"helping to preserve this country's legacy as a land of opportunity and freedom."*

"I can do all things through Christ who strengthens me." As you will read, my Christian faith plays an integral role in my life. My faith in God guides my decisions, both professionally and personally. Below, I have imparted the wisdom I have gained from God-given family (primarily my mother and brother) and friends, in hopes that you will live a fulfilled life.

It's Okay to be the "Underdog."

Law school was quite difficult for me. I didn't know any attorneys and had never worked in a law firm. Reading a law firm textbook that contained legalese was like reading a foreign language. I struggled to read *one* case study, which took me over 1 hour - the allotted time to complete four to five case studies. On the first day of class, I didn't even know that readings were assigned. Then there was the "Socratic" method which was terrifying. I was a pariah because I was always "one step behind." I watched as study group formed all around me.

However, once I caught my stride, I not only ended up landing a paid internship after my first year, but I also graduated in 2½ years, which enabled me to sit the Bar and start working one semester early.

Don't Compete and Don't Compare.

Don't compete with anyone, but yourself. If you see someone along the way who is struggling, help them. You never know when they will be of help to you. Don't compare yourself to anyone else - you have only what you have. Capitalize on what you do have. I may not be the most knowledgeable or experienced immigration attorney, but I have a lot of heart, creativity, passion, and unceasing work ethic, a lethal combination of skills that I use to win my cases. I also have God, who gives me legal strategies while I am falling asleep, or in the office, or at court.

Just Try. There's More than One Way to "Skin a Cat."

One of the things that I love about practicing immigration law is that I get to make creative arguments. My best clients are those whose backs are against the proverbial wall. Why? Because since they have no other choice, they are "in it, to win it." There was even one time, where I had given up, but my client told me, "Go ahead. I want you to try." With that, I gave it my very best effort, and ended up winning the case.

Be Humble. Be Grateful.

I try to stay grounded. Although I am extremely blessed, I could lose it all in a second. During my final exams of my first year of law school, my mother had a heart attack. I immediately took a leave of absence and abruptly left my internship to be by her side. Thankfully, she made a full recovery, but I remember putting my forehead to the ground making promises to God to spare her life. Today, every day on my way to work, I thank God for all my blessings - health, family, friends, my practice/home/cars, my dog, etc.

Never Give Up. Hard Work and Sacrifice Pays Off.

On my wall, I have the phrase, "if it doesn't challenge you, it doesn't change you." Don't stop when faced with adversity. We all face challenges on a daily basis. Remember that "nothing changes, if nothing changes." When I started my law firm, I worked from home and ate one meal a day comprised of rice and Indian pickle. Today, I have a thriving law firm.

Always Do More Than What is Required.

When I was growing up and my older brother, Roger taught me "always do more than what is required" and "do your job and someone else's." I believe that my firm is successful because I never do the minimum.

* * *

Dawn C. Sequeira, Esq.
Owner and Principal Attorney
Legacy Immigration, LLC
dawn@legacyimmigrationattorney.com
www.legacyimmigrationattorney.com

Mallika Chopra

Mom, Media Entrepreneur
Founder: Intent.com
Author, Public Speaker

Mallika Chopra

BIOGRAPHY

Mallika Chopra is the Founder of Intent.com, a platform focused on personal, social and global wellness. She is also the Founder of The Chopra Well, a premiere YouTube channel, launched with her brother, Gotham Chopra, and father, Deepak Chopra.

Mallika's most recent book, **"Living With Intent: My Somewhat Messy Journey to Purpose, Peace and Joy,"** was published in April 2015. Her earlier books, "100 Promises To My Baby" and "100 Questions From My Child" have been translated and sold in dozens of countries worldwide.

Her varied background includes launching the Heal The World Foundation in the 1990's with Michael Jackson, being part of re-launching MTV in India, and Health Ambassador for the Pepsi Refresh Everything Project in the US — an initiative that gave millions of dollars to individuals, non-profits, and companies for projects in their communities.

Mallika has taught meditations to thousands of people. She enjoys speaking to audiences around the world, including TedX and the Women's Conferences. She has shared ideas on balance and purpose at many companies, including Coca Cola, Disney, LinkedIn and Google.

Her writings and work have been featured in many publications including Time.com, Self Magazine, Women's Health, Prevention Magazine, OWN, Glamour, Oprah.com, Mind Body Green, the LA Times, and Huffington Post. She currently is featured in Time Magazine's Special Issue on Mindfulness.

Mallika has a Bachelor of Arts from Brown University, an MBA from Kellogg Business School, and is presently pursuing a Masters in Psychology with mind/ body/ spirit concentration at Teachers College, Columbia University.

How to Let Love In
the Power of Coincidence and Following Your Heart

by Mallika Chopra

"I am responsible for what I see. I choose the feelings I experience and set the goals I will achieve. Everything that seems to happen to me, I ask for and receive as I have asked. What do YOU ask for?"

When I was 23, I moved from Boston to New Delhi for a dream job. I was launching MTV India, learning all aspects of media and sales, and I had a business card that could get me into any nightclub. But there was one caveat to taking the position: I had to move into my grandparents' home.

I had grown up in Boston in a fairly modern Indian family— including my father, Deepak Chopra. Our life had involved its fair share of Indian tradition, but I had also been given a lot of independence. When I got to New Delhi, there were some noticeable changes, and some were easier to embrace than others. Respect for my elders was part of my upbringing, so I accepted the constant oversight and loving concern of my grandparents even if it felt unnecessary. My grandmother waited for me to come home every night, making it difficult for me to stay out after 10 P.M. I also didn't dare to wear a skirt above my knees, and I was careful about who I invited home—particularly boys. Being a grown adult, I certainly felt like it was taking a step back in time.

Despite coming from a liberal family, I knew my parents secretly hoped I would meet a nice Indian boy and "settle down." They never said it explicitly, and our family did not

127

believe in arranged marriages, but I knew that everyone was on the lookout for an appropriate match for me. They wanted me to end up with someone kind, smart, and stable. And they hoped I would get married early, like they did, and build my life with someone.

I had a very different mind-set. I was ambitious, and I knew I wanted to return to the U.S. for graduate school and explore every opportunity my education and blessed upbringing had afforded me. My interests at age 23 were freedom, having fun, and learning as much as I could. I felt marriage would force me to slow down, take away my independence, and steal from me the excitement life had to yet offer.

On my first day in New Delhi, my cousin hosted a "graffiti party" where everyone wore white and used washable markers to draw on one another. I felt shy and out of place at first but was quickly engulfed by the festive atmosphere. People were having fun and laughing, and within minutes my white shirt was full of words, colors, and drawings. During the free-for-all, I noticed one particular guy—tall, dark, and handsome, he was hard to miss. In the chaos, we spoke for just a minute, and by night's end, I couldn't even remember his name.

The next day I washed my T-shirt. Most of the colors disappeared, save for one distinct mark—in black ink, the name **Sumant** remained on the upper left corner. The name just wouldn't wash away.

What Happened Next

A friend invited me to dinner that night, and among the guests was the same handsome guy I'd seen at the party.

"Mallika, this is Sumant," my friend said. I couldn't help but smile. You're the indelible-marker guy," I said, and explained what had happened with my T-shirt. Sumant revealed that he had borrowed a pen from a friend when he saw me, and my shirt was the only one he'd written on. Turns out, it was a permanent marker.

As the evening progressed, Sumant and I got to know each other. He was a pragmatic engineer who had gone to college in the U.S. and returned to India to work in his family business. There was something so real and grounding about him, and we found that we had numerous family connections and similarities. As we spoke, my heart beat faster with excitement, but also, I felt anxious. I knew immediately that Sumant was the man my parents and family had hoped I would meet. I felt myself resisting the desire to get to know him better, as if that would be their dream, not mine, and that marriage could change so many hopes that I had for my future.

But having grown up with Deepak Chopra as a father, I was taught to be open and always ask questions. I reflected on the signs the universe was sending me. Could anything be more obvious than Sumant written above my heart in permanent ink? I decided to take a leap of faith, to trust my intuition, and to open myself completely to him.

Within two weeks, we both knew this was our lifelong relationship. We dated quietly for another four months, not ready to tell our families just yet. Despite living in the U.S. and feeling like a modern couple, we were both still respectful of the traditions of our families and knew that once we shared the news of our relationship, marriage would be inevitable. It may seem strange to some, but as traditions in our culture go, this was the only path to take. Eventually, about a year after we met, we did get married — in a memorable and extravagant Indian wedding.

Sumant and I remained committed to our personal and professional intents. We returned to the U.S. and both completed our M.B.A.s at Kellogg Business School. We gave each other the freedom and space to pursue our goals, which required living in separate cities for months at a time. But we were committed to growing up together and supporting each other on our individual and combined journeys.

Now, 20 years after we first met, Sumant and I remain happily married and have two incredible daughters, Tara and Leela. I believe more strongly than ever that the universe was gently guiding me toward my future husband all along. If I hadn't believed in the power of coincidence and kept my mind and heart open to signs, I might have missed out on living the full life I'm so lucky to have today.

In closing, I share with you a road map on how to live with more intent – from my new book, *"Living with Intent: My Somewhat Messy Journey to Purpose, Peace and Joy."*

INCUBATE: Quiet your mind to tap into your deepest intentions; see where this leads.

NOTICE: Become mindful of your thoughts and actions and

pay attention to what they tell you about what gives you meaning and a sense of purpose – and look for signs that can point you towards your truth.

TRUST: Have confidence in your inner knowing – and in the messages the universe sends you – and allow that knowledge to guide you forward.

EXPRESS: Write down your intentions; say them out loud or share them with others to fully embrace them and help you move ahead in your journey.

NURTURE: Be gentle with yourself as you try to find your way. Intention isn't always a straightforward path, just like life, and giving yourself opportunities to try – and fail – is often part of, and even crucial to, the process.

TAKE ACTION: Once you've identified an intent, or even multiple ones, don't sit and wait for it to magically manifest; instead take the practical steps that can make each become a reality. It may be easiest to choose one intent first and set short-term goals to help you get started.

In my book, "**Living with Intent,**" I share my personal stories, research, practical tips and exercises for each of these six steps. When you order it, you also receive a free gift of my eBook *"Meditation with Mallika Chopra"*. You are invited to share this offer with any and everyone! Namaste.

* * *

Mallika Chopra
Founder: Intent.com
www.mallikachopra.com

Traci Clarida

Change Facilitator, Coach
Owner: Let's Get "Stuff" Done

BIOGRAPHY

Influenced by Deepak Chopra's writings on leadership, Traci chose "inspire" as her mantra. Traci is inspired to raise people up, to help them see their unique abilities and gifts, and to empower them to believe in themselves and accomplish the hard things.

Traci has a firm belief that the world needs more love, compassion, and optimism. She strives to be the kind of person whose energy is contagious and spreads positivity to those around her, creating an environment of trust and confidence. She lends this environment to her company Let's Get "Stuff" Done, LLC, a life coaching business that offers change facilitation for women who are ready to break free from undesirable thought and behavior patterns.

Traci strives to create a compelling vision for her clients to help them see the heart of the matter, implement steps to overcome obstacles and complete goals, and execute solid plans for success. By inspiring her clients, Traci is able to help them triumph over their lack of motivation or direction, helping them to get "stuff" done.

Having conquered many personal obstacles, Traci is a master at applying her own life lessons. She views every situation as a way to learn more about herself and the world around her, imbuing her with wisdom to help her clients. She has learned to laugh at her mistakes, forgive herself for imperfection, and embrace self-forgiveness and self-acceptance – three key concepts she teaches in her e-book, "Finding Your 'Right' Way: Three Practices for Self-Discovery".

Traci has Bachelor and Master of Science degrees in Psychology and is a licensed massage therapist.

Questing for Authenticity

by Traci Clarida

"When standing still becomes more uncomfortable than fear of the unknown – this is when you know you are ready to make changes and get 'stuff' done."

Are you on a quest for a happy life? A life well-lived? An authentic and genuine existence? Me too! Living authentic lives in harmony with our true natures sounds simple but is actually quite challenging, especially when we realize the way we've been living is no longer bringing peace to our souls. When we're drowning in unhappiness and self-loathing, we gain a keen awareness that we must make changes before our souls suffocate.

Significant life changes often require moving away from our cultural, religious, or spiritual traditions, and the safety and security we feel from striving toward an "ideal" or "perfection." It opens doors to formerly forbidden freedom that is exciting yet lonely at the same time. It creates a vacuum that begs to be filled but with what does one fill it? I suggest new knowledge (sometimes mixed with former knowledge), freedom from self-judgment, and a hearty sense of humor.

Stepping out of my "box" and onto the path of my genuine self, meant leaving the belief system in which I was raised to discover my own. I found a combination of what I was taught as a girl mixed with a few concepts from various religions and philosophies is what "works" for me. The only way you will know what "works" for you is to give yourself space to experiment. Read a lot and try a few different practices. Do they make you feel good? Give yourself permission to try something and discard it if you find it's not what you truly believe. Be willing to use an idea or philosophy for a while until it no longer fulfills its purpose in your life, then send it to the bin. The evolution of your beliefs will evolve and change as you do, and that is a good thing!

Traci Clarida

One of my favorite sayings, most often attributed to Ian Maclaran, is "Everyone you meet is fighting a battle you know nothing about. Be kind. Always." This includes being nice to yourself. Not only must we give ourselves room to experiment with our beliefs, we must afford ourselves the same benefit of the doubt we would a stranger who inadvertently wrongs us. This includes foregoing judgment when we make choices that don't bring us a desired result.

It is likely we will bumble about a bit in our journey for an authentic life. This is normal! You and I are allowed to draw a line in the sand as many times as we want. Shed yourself of former beliefs that purport a penance must be paid for poor or wrong choices, and instead cut yourself some slack. It takes a long time to undo a lifetime of training. If you find yourself in old patterns of thinking that don't support your ideals of who you are becoming, gently acknowledge this to yourself, and move on. There is no need for self-punishment or disappointment because you are perfectly okay simply being you!

As you mature in your ability to avoid self-judgment, your capacity for self-forgiveness will naturally increase. When you give up the idea of perfection and stop striving for it, you will gain the confidence to laugh at yourself rather than criticize. Even when your mistakes seem unforgivable, you can learn from them and start anew. Humor is the balm that will sooth your soul and give you courage to journey on.

It is scary to make changes and venture into the unknown; however, you are more equipped than you realize. A simple evaluation of what you already know, a choosing of that which you still believe, and a hunger to learn new ideas are all you need to get started. There will be challenges, including relinquishment of self-judgment, but as you learn to exercise humor you will discover someone definitely worth knowing – your authentic self!

* * *

Traci Clarida
Owner
Let's Get "Stuff" Done
info@letsgetstuffdone.com
385-323-0509
www.letsgetstuffdone.com

135

CHANGE

Realize who you are -
Become what you must.
Though the newness
May seem strange.

Meet today with courage
Tomorrow trust,
As you welcome
The challenge of change.

Something new may be meeting a need,
and needs change as one grows,
Many a change transforms a seed
Before it becomes a rose.

But if the seed were to shrink from the sun,
And cling instead to the earth.
The bud would never be begun,
Nor could the rose find birth.

Don't cling with fear to the tried and true,
Remember: it too, once was new.
Greet life eagerly, ever knowing -
Ever changing - is ever growing.

© Pat Sampson

Ana Weber

Speaker, Innovator
Bestselling Author

Ana Weber

BIOGRAPHY

Ana Weber is the founder of anaweberdoxa.com, introducing **"THE DOXA METHOD"**. The DOXA Method is a success formula Ana Implemented for over 26 years, in the process she elevated business success and influenced senior leaders and overall company culture.

Ana's passion is to empower people to transport their fears into success and furthermore to learn how to let go of past emotional baggage, (extract the seeds of wisdom) accomplish remarkable results in the present, enjoy the "NOW" and move forward with dreams, goals and ideas with liberty and personal freedom.

Ana was born in Romania under communism regime, experiencing scarcity and tremendous emotional and fearful challenges. Relocating to Israel with her Mother, Ana at age 10 learned the facts of life, from her very first assignment collecting chicken eggs on the farm, to embracing a new language and pursue education and adapt. Between tears and heartache she graduated high school Magna Cum laude.

Ana's business and leadership expertise and drive contributed to organizations growth such as Porsche Race Car Division, The Smithsonian Institute and the medical field, the launching of the first cpap, a revolutionary medical device saving the life of millions globally.

Ana published 5 best seller books translated into multiple languages globally and spreading the word. Often Ana receives an email from a student or an entrepreneur "You saved my life". Ana was featured extensively in USA Today, Wall Street Journal, and Huffington Post and appeared on ABC Radio, Rose Colombo and Business Weekly show.

She is deeply involved in helping and supporting organizations such as One Woman Fearless, The Unstoppable Foundation, and Women of Global Change.

Ana pursued continued education at Oxford University with a Ph.D in philosphy and an MBA from Ashford University. Throughout her career and education Ana adopted and practices daily a huge profound quote: "Even a rock wants to feel important".

From Fear to Success!

Feel! Time!

by Ana Weber

"Even a rock wants to feel important"

I was born in Romania under Communism regime. Throughout my childhood I experienced tremendous life challenges and circumstances. I was shy, insecure and totally sheltered from the world. In actuality I never felt like a child. I felt the burdens of life landing on my shoulders, feeling fearful to speak up or express my emotions. I felt anxious and distant.

At the age of 10 my Mother and I immigrated to the Middle East to find liberty and opportunities. You can imagine how challenging this move was. Transitioning from a city life filled with culture but poor to a life that we were unfamiliar with. We had to adjust to a new style of living and due to circumstances I joined a farm/school where only poor children and orphans were accepted. I shared a room with 3 other girls and a bathroom down the hall with 12 other girls. I can still recall the fear and sadness I encountered while working on my very first assignment.

I was asked by my supervisor that I had to meet the daily quota; collecting 150 chicken eggs in 3 hours. My story is heartwarming and inspirational. The first few days, I collected only 30-eggs. Out of fear, intimidation and the sad newness, missing the life I was accustomed to and especially the presence of Mom I failed meeting the expected quota. But after a few days of dissapointments I decided to get over my fears and meet the assignment. I had no idea how this transformation will take place and out of sheer fear on the 5th day I entered the chicken cage areas and proceeded to sing a familiar aria touching on my past; LA DONNA MOBILE from the Opera, Rigoletto. To my suprise my singing brought on a huge shift. The chickens calmed down and walked back regally to their cages. With the awareness of a 10 year old girl, I was able to meet the quota and go over and beyond.

And life began to taste sweet as Mom and I encountered a few miracles and transformed our life from rags to riches.

Moving fast forward, at 23, my family and I immigrated again to start a new life in the U.S.A. and live our dream and goals. I pursued a business degree and a powerful career in finance. I filled top executive positions such as CFO, CEO, VP of sales for medium to large organizations. I began to believe in myself, the awesome purpose I felt passionate about, (people) and empower people to be at their best, be unstoppable and in the course of her life I was instrumental in creating business success for many organizations and raise the human mind with personal development and leadership courage.

The message I shared with hundreds of people globally and never to give up! NEVER to give in just practice the "giving more"and create extra ordinary results and success.

Going through major life experiences I marched against all odds and became a world renowed success authoring 17 books, 1 work book and 1 complete course. I speak, lecture and conduct work shops globally and fear was dropped off along the journey. With each and every step of the way driving my life vehicle, I let go of my insecurities, shyness and fear, replacing and replenishing it with courage, enthusiasm, and tremendous passion. I engage audiences and create a warm and close relationship with attendees, corporate executives, entrepreneurs and students. With authentic and genuine life stories, making the impossible to possible I empower people to walk away with golden nuggets they can tailor to fit their needs and inspire others by their accomplished successful results impacted by the wisdom of choice.

Moving fast forward I am delighted to continue my path and influence the world to live a full happy and meaningful. life.

I became deeply intrigued and passionate about money and money management, so I pursued a higher education in business and entered into the corporate world. It was a phenomenal world and everyday when I encountered obstacles and internal culture and need for growth I got more and more excited. The opportunities to rise and speak up were amazing and I discovered a whole new person. Ana the relationship expert and negotiator. With great leadership and training others we all grew and business took a whole new angle.

All business juices were flowing beautifully up to 2006 when life presented a huge personal challenge and change.

I had so many questions; Why? Why me? Why now? And with a new transformation and ideas I merged into a whole new field; philosophy and psychology. I need a deeper understanding of why certain things change so dramatically? Why people are not accountable? What makes people change so much?

And life took a whole new spin. I enrolled into philosphy and psychology classes and pursued additional education. I began writing and writing felt magic. One book after the other, expressing all that I felt, experienced and empowered others and life felt sweet and free. I wrote papers and one of my books served as the thesis prior to graduating.

Who would have believed, that little girl from Romania made a huge leap and nothing stopped her from pursuing her dreams, Dreams have no expiration date attached to them.

I am thrilled and excited beyond words sharing my philosophy, my outlook on life, people and the world.

MY Personal Philosophy

Since I was a young child I had a dual relationship with philosophy. What made perfect sense, what seemed like an illusion? Or not? And what place does the experience or the fundamental realistic facts represent? Learning about Socrates and Carl Jung and other influential philosophers I began to develop a passion and a tremendous drive to dissect and understand philosophy but more so to navigate and shift my personal philosophy and create a sincere desire to share my findings and personal experiences and triumphs with the world.

141

Practicing and living my personal philosophy led me to publish my latest book, **"THE DOXA METHOD"**: *Transport your fears into success.* Isn't fear stopping us from stepping from unfamiliarity to familiarity? **The answer is loud and clear.** We cannot change feelings. Your feelings belong to you. Validating your feelings is the first step to building healthy and lasting relationships. I call it **"filtering"**. Only with more logic and blending feelings with common sense do we reach an amicable resolution.

My personal philosophy fundamental rule is all about the value and the profound meaning to *"feel time"* and stop *"filling time"*. When you feel time, you enter a whole new dimension of what is important? Where would you like to be tomorrow and share your big moment with?

Love life, love more and never stop loving! Life will love you back unconditionally. Life is on standby at your personal station, hop on and enjoy! On a recent survey hundreds of people were asked what they would like to change in their lives: Get higher education? Make more money? Travel more? A bigger house? Stop aging? The shocking results showed one simple sentence "I wish I spent more time with my loved ones and use more often the three word powerful sentence: "**I LOVE YOU**".

* * *

Ana Weber
949-422-1830
ana@anaweberdoxa.com
www.anaweberdoxa.com

Paula Neva Vail

TV/Radio Host, Author
Reiki Master/Teacher

Paula Neva Vail

BIOGRAPHY

Paula Neva Vail, Owner of Wellness Inspired, is recognized nationally as a powerful advocate of personal empowerment. From customers to friends, from brief interactions to professional connections, Paula's greatest gift is to inspire others, and in so doing, helps make this world a better and happier place.

Prior to her Reiki practice and radio show, Paula was Manager/Owner of a popular Tacoma area restaurant for 27 years. Paula's sunny disposition and tenacious spirit created an environment that kept customers coming back for great food, friendly service, and a jolt of positive energy.

"Positive energy can and will help others in a plethora of different ways, but just like everything else, there is a process to using it and cultivating it." She brought her talents to radio, hosting the first internet talk radio show on *Voice America*: "For the Love of Reiki." She hosted the show more than two years and loved every moment. In 2015, she expanded to other networks and TV, re-naming the show: **"Choices: Finding your Joy", on Seattle, AM Radio 1150KKNW,** as well as You Tube.

Paula was featured in New York City's Times Square by Continental Who's Who as a Pinnacle Professional. Among awards too numerous to mention, Paula was honored for life and business achievements --- twice by Women of Distinction Magazine -- 2015 edition -- and the cover story of the 2017 edition; in 2018, Paula was featured on CUTV News in NYC., as well as a feature story in "ICE" Magazine. Paula was honored "Top Wellness Coach of Year 2017"; and "Top Female Professional of 2018" by the International Association of Top Professionals; and "Best of Tacoma" in the Wellness category for three consecutive years.

Paula's core beliefs are chronicled in her upcoming book, "Why Am I So Happy?" She is also active in charity work throughout the USA and the world, in hopes of making a difference in the welfare of people and animals.

"Why Am I So Happy?"

The Sign of true success is a happy heart!
by Paula Neva Vail

> "Character is how you treat someone
> who can do nothing for you "

"Why am I so happy?" I am asked – over and over – for as long as I remember. It may be the big smile on my face, sharing a kind word with someone, or spontaneously dancing to a song. I have these joyous moments without thinking why I feel such joy.

Happiness is my natural state of being and my birthright. I welcome each opportunity to express it. This does not mean there aren't times that I must consciously reject negative thoughts and choose to smile by reflecting on all the good things in my life -- for which there are many.

I have seen tragedy and experienced sadness just like every other person. I faced challenges with strength from the very day I came into this world. I was born premature weighing less than 3 pounds. My anxious parents were told I would probably not survive the night. I must have had a strong will to live, even then, for I not only survived in good health but thrived.

145

I greet each new day with a sense of curiosity and innate drive. Each moment filled with gratitude that it is mine. Things could have turned out much differently and that knowledge sparks my life with a strong sense of purpose. I believed early on that I would do something great with the life I have been given against all odds. And, for those interim moments when a word of encouragement is needed, I think of how others persisted in the face of utter discouragement and it renews my spirit. I long to do the same for others.

I will share with you some of the tools to opening the door to happiness that resides naturally in each and every one of us. It can be triggered or tapped in various ways. Joy creates a beautiful energy from within and is transferable to others, proving that one person can make a difference. Whatever your background, history or circumstances, you walk out the door free to make new choices, develop a positive attitude, and manifest your heart's desire.

Emotional Triggers

We consciously choose our thoughts. As you ask and feel and believe, you activate what I call emotional triggers. Example: If you focus on difficulties you have experienced, you draw more difficult circumstances to you. If, you however, see yourself with the freedom and empowerment to make a new start, this triggers happiness and unleashes the magic.

You are the only one who can create the life you deserve. If you focus on what you want, the law of attraction will manifest your goals, triggering excitement, joy and creativity.

If we focus on gratitude we trigger a loving, happy feeling that permeates our whole being. Gratitude triggers are spurred in many ways -- by the people we care about, family, friends, co-workers, pets, possessions, weather, scenery, wildlife, beauty, art, music, projects, health, or accomplishments. The list is endless.

Ask yourself: **What percentage of my day is focused on the positives rather than the negatives in my life?** Live in the moment. It is important to acknowledge the past, and though you may occasionally draw upon memories and experiences for inspiration, never idolize it at the risk of creating a backward drift in spite of all efforts to advance.

It is important to acknowledge the future, while opening the door to NOW. Now offers joy in the present moment, creating memories and excitement for the future. Now is the time to open our hearts to self-love, love and compassion for others. Now is the time to honor our physical body; feeling a connection to others, the animal kingdom, and mother earth. You discover all things are one and that awareness triggers happiness that attracts to you the desires of your heart.

"You alone control your happiness"

There is reason for good cheer. What you can be and do is largely determined by the attitude you hold most of the time. Attitude is a state of mind that grows until it circles itself with images of its own likeness. Your attitude reflects how you look at life, whether you see it as vibrant, exciting, busy, full of vivid impressions and new experiences, or whether it needs shining with a positive mental attitude.

The sign of true success is a happy heart! Celebrate the gift of life! Find joy in your accomplishments. Be grateful for all you have accomplished and all you will accomplish. Gratitude is a beautiful joyous gift. When we love and appreciate ourselves and others for the beautiful individuals we all are, we become a beacon of love and inspiration—lighting the way for others. How fantastic! What can be better than that?

* * *

Paula Neva Vail
Owner
Wellness Inspired
paula@wellnessinspired.com
www.wellnessinspired.com

Ingrid Laederach Steven

Owner: Swiss-Master Chocolatier

'Beautiful Chocolates to Beautiful People'

Ingrid Laederach Steven

BIOGRAPHY

Ingrid Laederach Steven, Owner of Swiss Master Chocolatier Shop is a woman of great personal warmth. You can't help feeling that you are in the company of a dear friend.

To Ingrid her upscale chocolate shop located in the prestigious Bridle Path area of Toronto, Canada is not just a business, but a *"Love story of a different kind"*.

Ingrid, born and raised in Switzerland, had the voice of an opera singer (plus an IQ of 180) that earned her two scholarships from the United States, where she appeared on television and travelled the country performing. Suddenly, an illness kept the rising star in a comma for two weeks, damaging her vocal chords, and ending a promising career.

Ingrid re-located to Toronto, Canada, met and married her amazing husband Tom, and together looked forward to starting a family. After seven heartbreaking miscarriages, a team of medical professionals performed a medical miracle (recorded in medical journals) that led to the birth of two beautiful daughters, Jaclyn and Jasmin.

A devoted mother and wife, her entrepreneurial spirit ignited when the opportunity arose to become the owner of Swiss-Master Chocolatier, selling "Beautiful Chocolates to Beautiful People", to some of the wealthiest and most influential people in Canada, including deliveries to the Queen Mother, and the Pope's entourage.

Clearly, Ingrid is doing everything right, as Swiss-Master Chocolatier is celebrating its 33rd anniversary with a congratulatory message from the Prime Minister of Canada. Ingrid has also been awarded "Retailer of the Year" by the Toronto Chamber of Commerce, and her life story receives mass recognition from Canadian, United States, and Swiss media.

At a time when stories of everday heroes are in short supply, her *"Beautiful Person of the Year"* site recognizes people - young and old -living under tremendously challenging circumstances - and those who strive to give back in any way possible. **The site receives over a million hits a year.**

It's All About Relationships

Love, Friendship and Chocolate

by Ingrid Laederach Steven

"I've learned that people will forget what you said, people will forget what you did, but people will never forget how you made them feel."
Maya Angelou

I BELIEVE that the happiest people are those who have found a profession they love and have created a loving family who supports and helps create and define the dream we all live for.

It is our experiences with other people that give our lives joy, meaning, and purpose. Our relationships affect our lives more than anything else. Caring family and friends are probably the highest incentives an individual can have on the road to making one's contribution to the world. Naturally, it is up to each and everyone of us to create the atmosphere of harmony and happiness where it all happens.

The message that has molded my outlook on both life and business centers around treating others with the same respect that you would treat a family member, which will ultimately position you to succeed. Growing up, I always knew I wanted to have a wonderful marriage and children, and I wanted to own my own business which would allow me the freedom to chart my own course in life.

When the opportunity presented itself to become the owner of Swiss Master Chocolatier, I knew it was exactly what I had been waiting for; truly the perfect fit for me! The business model was an exact match with my ideals, as it meant I would be in touch with people every day, and in turn, could build one-on-one relationships that would become an intricate part of my success.

151

'Beautiful Chocolates to Beautiful People'is more than a slogan, or a physical description. The most "beautiful people" I have known are those who have known defeat, known suffering, known struggle, known loss and have found their way out of the depths. These people have an appreciation, a sensitivity, and an understanding of life that fills them with compassion, gentleness, and a deep loving concern.

And everybody loves chocolates! Scientific studies have found chocolate to have many benefits very few other foods can complete with. Chocolates have always had a mystique and magic about them with an ability to ignite joy and happiness, if but for a lingering moment. For a 'male courting a love' bringing an 'I Love You' truffle can be a magical gift that is worth its weight in gold! (Swiss Master Chocolatier, 'fresh cream' truffles live up to this image.)

To me, the most powerful measure of my success is my reputation not only for having the best Swiss Chocolates in the world., but for treating others the way I wish to be treated- *living the Golden Rule.* If your customers feel you care about them, they will trust you, buy from you, and be loyal to you.

Over the years, aside from building up an amazing wonderful loyal clientele, we have many visits by world celebrities, sport stars, politicians, even astronauts. On any day you see Mercedes, BMWs and Hummers in the parking lot -- or stretched - limos -- and/or many world celebrities inside the store waiting patiently in line, happily chatting with others.

At first, when the late great Prince came to the store he was accompanied by his entourage and people lined up outside of the store in awe. Soon, prince began "dropping in" alone once he realized that everyone at Swiss Master Chocolatier, is treated as a VIP. This put him at ease and he totally loved being just 'another customer' walking around joking with all of us. Jon Voight is exceptionally interesting and friendly. One Easter, after he wrapped up one of his latest films, he came in and brought up all our chocolate Easter bunnies for the entire crew!

Yes, celebrities from all over the world are a constant part of our story, certainly, but the most rewarding aspects of coming to work every day, is seeing the familiar faces, asking about their families, their success, and their challenges, sharing stories and catching up. Smiles and hugs. Rejoicing in the good times and offering support in dark times. Is it any wonder so many of our customers are friends?

It's so important to communicate and interact with people, and show that you care. It's as simple as that. Greet everyone with a warm smile. No matter how busy you are. See how different it makes you feel. When I start my day smiling, it sparks a positive attitude, optimism, enthusiasm and cheerfulness. I am so very thankful for all of my blessings. Especially for all the people I love, and who love me.

I am so blessed. My husband, Tom, has been at my side through all the years - the man who would change my life forever. What touched me about Tom was his kindness and honesty. And he was good looking to boot! I knew he was the right man for me when on the way to a dance, he abruptly stopped the car, and helped a handicapped and partially-blind person cross the street. To say I was overwhelmed, is putting it mildly. I was hooked full line and sinker. I knew then he would make a wonderful husband and a great father.

Tom is always there for me through the good times and the sad times. He comforted me during seven miscarriages when I sometimes lost all hope. And the immense joy shared on the birth of two beautiful daughters, Jasmin and Jaclyn, (who have given us four amazing grandchildren) is beyond description. And on top of all that!- a business that has thrived for 33years with customers who are like extended family. *Who could ask for anything more?*

My experiences make it clear to me, that there is always hope for the future. We are where we are today - in the present - as a result of what we have experienced in the past. We build on our experiences to find out who we are and what we are made of.

We dream our own dreams, and then hopefully, by taking action and by keeping hope alive, we can make a difference in the lives of others.

Live every day grateful that it is yours. Enjoy every moment. Be happy for all that you have, and don't waste your time thinking about what you do not have. Do whatever makes you the happiest. If selling and making floral arrangements versus going up the academic ladder is what makes you happy, then that is what you should be doing.

Set goals. The journey is what makes it all worthwhile and memorable. Go on the journey, but be prepared that there can be potholes along the way. Jump over them or walk around them. Make all the separate and unique pieces fit together. Love yourself even more for not giving up. Cultivate a positive attitude to serve and protect you through the rough patches. It will help you get to those moments when you can smile without forcing it, concentrate without faking it, and laugh like you mean it.

Believe in yourself. Believe in other people. Believe that if you work hard, give of yourself honestly, and are sincere, obstacles can be overcome. You can make your dreams come true.

Today is a beautiful day. Be Positive. Be Optimistic. Be Enthusiastic. Do the right things for the right reasons and smile. The rest will fall into place with a dose of optimism, and hope - *and a few chocolates.*

* * *

Ingrid Laederach Steven
416-444-8802
Ingridswiss@gmail.com
www.swissmaster.com

F.R.I.E.N.D.S
Love you.
Respect you.
Encourage you.
Support your Dreams.
Believe in you.
Need you.
Deserve you.
Stand by you.

Punky and Crickett

Michaelee Jenkins

Mother • Entrepreneur • Designer

Broker Owner, RE/MAX Homes
Co Founder and Owner: My Time Yoga Studio

Michaelee Jenkins

BIOGRAPHY

Michaelee Jenkins is an exceptional woman. She earned her reputation as an astute industry leader through a great amount of talent and know-how, love of people, a strong positive attitude and determination to succeed.

From 14 to 29, Michaelee worked 30+ jobs --- full time, part time, and weekends -- a schedule only the most ambitious and energetic could endure – and opened networks of opportunities that would come to serve her professional life.

Michaelee married Tim in 1991 and together they opened a fast food enterprise. Living with fibromyalgia, Michaelee knew it would not last long term. At 38, with her husband's full support, she began her real estate career and within three years was honored as a multi-million dollar producer. Tim joined her and together built one of the most respected "teams" west of Minneapolis; recognized in the top 2% of Minneapolis MLS closed transactions. In 2006, Michaelee was inducted into the RE/MAX International Hall of Fame. The same year, she became CEO of Team Jenkins RE Inc., and Broker Owner of RE/MAX Homes in Glencoe, MN.

Michaelee's winning spirit is the basis of a life lived with hopefulness and meaning. Devoted to family, and the business she loves, she is "living the life she imagined". Not resting on her laurels, Michaelee became a certified yoga instructor, owns a yoga studio, and teaches clients the benefits of relaxation, proper breathing, and living mindfully.

Michaelee loves gardening and the tropics, and her property is surrounded with hundreds of canna lilies, caster bean, elephant ears, and various unique treasures. At age 55, she began playing the cello and stays active walking, bicycling, golfing and traveling the world with her family.

DARE TO BE DIFFERENT

Free Your Mind from Perfection

by Michaelee Jenkins

"Free Your Mind from Perfection; Free Your Heart from Worry; Live Simple; Give More; Expect Less."

I grew up as a kid "loaded" with energy. To this day, I still get people wishing they had half the energy I have. At times, it can be embarrassing, because sometimes I don't know how to be quiet when I become so excited I interrupt people while they are talking! In my late 20's I started practicing yoga. Then, I began to learn how to manage my enthusiasm when necessary.

Yoga has taught me how to live in the moment and not "worry" about the "what ifs" in life. I learned to "breathe" into my body and remain calm through the chaotic times of feeling anxious. I learned to be mindful of what is happening around me and to stay into control. It's okay to lose yourself in the moment and not worry about what you might miss out on saying, because it really doesn't matter. Stay humble. If it's meant to be said, you will remember it.

To reach a goal you must build trust and relationships with people. No one cares about how much you know, only that you care. Challenge yourself to become a better person by going outside your comfort zone and learning something new. Become a better listener and show compassion. Look others in the eye as they share -- it builds trust. This has helped our business grow through referrals from happy clients throughout many years.

Always, take time to keep yourself healthy and happy, because it is essential in helping others achieve their dreams. You must feel good to send healthy vibrations to others. Always remember no one is perfect and that no one wants to deal with someone who thinks they know it all. The ego can spoil relationships in a hurry, try hard not to make it yours.

158

Free your Heart from Worry

Success begins at home. We all have memories – good and bad -- from the way we were raised. Take control and own who you are and who you want to become. Make necessary changes in your life. Create your own fashion and become who you want to be right now. Live the life you have imagined!

Be careful what you watch and how you think. The Law of Attraction is working in your life, whether you acknowledge it or not. You reap what you sow. You are the maker and producer of your own life's movie. No one succeeds without failing so don't worry about yesterday, it's gone. Learn from your mistakes and stay focused on your dream. To fail means that you are going outside your box and taking risks. This is a warrior trait that proves you are paving a path to success.

I always felt the more times you fail the closer you become to accomplishing your goal. Never forget to smell the roses along the way. Set goals and write them down. Recording them holds you accountable and makes things happen! There is nothing more fulfilling then to cross off each goal as they are achieved. It lightens the load with proof that you are moving forward while smelling the roses along the way!

Allow yourself to learn from your children. You are blessed having them in your life; and their powerful souls are yours to nourish with love and understanding. Find a true mission and purpose that really motivates you. This helps control your thoughts which results in positive action. Find time to pray. Honor special quiet time to listen to God's answers. Most importantly, be patient while He works on the shifts in consciousness that needs to take place first within you, in order to manifest your dreams.

Live Simple

Life doesn't have to be hard. Eliminate the things, relationships and events that no longer serve you. Work on building your self-esteem. By doing so, energy opens up that is so powerful it gives you additional internal space to "feel" more, and axiomatically makes you a happier person.

Purge, release past dramas, refuse to carry old burdens you no longer control----why damage your mental, emotional or physical state over past choices or the occurrences or actions of others? All of your life movie's episodes are controlled by you! Refuse to waste your energy blaming others for anything. Just own it and move forward becoming that beautiful creative soul you want to be!

Stay focused. It's so much easier to acknowledge that we do not know it all. A favorite personal policy of mine is to listen more than speak, because this is how we learn. Always keep an open mind to better yourself on a personal level. Respect the boundaries of others and treat other people exactly how you want them to treat you.

Success is never about how much money you make, what you own, or who you know. Remember who you are and who you want to become. You are the product of your belief system and thought patterns. If you allow your dreams and morals to guide you through life, it will lead you to becoming the warrior you need to be to manifest your deepest desires.

A true warrior doesn't need to be praised or reminded of every simple accomplishment you achieve because...you just know. In your own heart and mind, you "see" and live the result you imagine "right now". This keeps you happy and frees up energy to love others more – then -- watch the Law of Attraction return back to you ten-fold!

Give More • Expect Less

I remember the recession in 2008, I had to decide which bills to pay and which ones had to wait. I worked short sales because nothing traditional was moving. Daily, I watched bad things happen to good people. I watched fellow associates and bankers lose their homes. I battled with banks trying to save the devastating change about to play out in my client's lives I literally worked for free for over five years to save the company.

During this time of utter chaos, my dear mother shared some spiritual advice which led me to my yoga instructor and life coach. I attended a workshop "Awaken the Joy Within" January 1, 2013 which changed my life. One exercise was to create a vision board of all my loves in life. It didn't need to make sense, I just needed to do it.

September of that year, the "Sanctuary Health & Wellness Fund Raiser"manifested. For several years, we held a one-day event focused on alternative/holistic education providing other ways of healing than traditional medicine. All proceeds went to children with special needs.

The planning of this incredible event directed my "stinking thinking" into something so big and productive it changed the lives of many! It was one of the most rewarding dreams I ever experienced! My "movie of life" began to shift with a stream of miracles.

From this network of doctors, healers, and instructors, I developed lifelong relationships. Now, through a divine intervention, we have been introduced to a high tech physical vascular medical device and are, once again, off to another business venture in life. However, the most powerful day was when I became a mother, and by remaining approachable while nourishing others, keeps my ignited soul inspired by giving back into the world. *Namaste!*

* * *

Michaelee Jenkins, Broker/Owner
RE/MAX Homes - michaeleeremax@gmail.com
952-992-9299   www.teamjenkins.net
Co Founder/Owner: My Time Yoga Studio

Lori Kessler

Owner: Contractor Solutions

Project Manager, Mommy, 'Lola'

Lori Kessler

BIOGRAPHY

Ms. Kessler has over 27+ years of working in the heavy highway and bridge construction, civil engineering discipline. She began her career while living in Hawaii at age 20 working for an engineering company in administration. When she decided to leave the island, the Vice President of the company encouraged her to pursue a career in engineering. She returned to her Midwest home and continued her career with the local government engineering division. Following a decade of working there, she relocated to Maryland, where she currently resides.

Throughout her career, Ms. Kessler has held several positions from Engineering Associate, Project Manager and Sr. Project Engineer for civil infrastructure projects. Passionate and eager to expand her horizons, she extended her involvements in national associations. She authored engineering manuals for several State Department of Transportations' in a wide range of civil infrastructure disciplines(e.g.,highway maintenance and construction, roadway design, environment, traffic, state hydraulics and hydrology.) She has presented at conferences, been published in trade magazines/national newsletters, and gained recognition by winning a national award.

Some of her career affiliations and accomplishments: Member-"The Road Gang",Washington's Transportation Fraternity; Won - "National pavement for preservation Excellence Award,"FP² for Frederick County, Maryland; Co - Author - "Maryland Makes Preservation Work," Inside Maryland's Award - winning Pavement Plan, pp.26-28, Better Roads magazine, February 2007; Past Member - Asphalt Recycling and Reclaiming Association (ARRA) Presenter - "Incorporating Asphalt Recycling with Pavement Management Systems,"Florida;"Asphalt Recycling-An Agencies Perspective,"Pennsylvania and Ohio for ARRA; Past Affiliate-Transportation Research Board, Individual Associate and Friends of Committee AFD10 "Pavement Management Systems".

In 2016, Ms. Kessler began a new journey by starting her own business, **Contractor Solutions**. Her business assists contractors with project tasks to meet State DOTs Disadvantaged Business Enterprise(DBE) goal requirements(i.e., materials supply, construction/project management).

Construction Barbie

Crossing a bridge to endless dreams
by Lori Kessler

"Find Commonality with Others"

If the title "Construction barbie" is confusing you, it confused me as well. It was coined by my best friend who said, *"I can't believe what you do for a living, and you actually know what you're talking about."* So, it stuck. Aside from my career, my love of family is my true passion. I am blessed with two adult teenagers and two grandchildren (they know me as Lola). I was fortunate to be raised by four parents whose individual strengths were instrumental in building my character and self-worth. All of this has guided me along the way and has made me feel accomplished and proud of my achievements.

My mother is one of the most intelligent women I know. She was a single-mother of three for most of my youth. Her solid work ethic provided for my siblings and me. I have seen her repair appliances, garage doors, fences, windows, and almost anything that was broken or inoperable. Her common every-day life struggles were real. For example, the luxury of having toilet paper in the house was nearly non-existent. Fortunately, we lived next to a laundromat, so we would simply take their toilet paper. It's a common joke for anyone that knows me. If I'm down to 7 rolls of toilet paper, I panic and immediately get to the store to restock the supply.

My father was a private man with great character. He was meticulous and detailed with any project/task he undertook. He told me he could never build a house. Explaining, it would have to be square and if he couldn't get it perfect, he wouldn't shimmy the angles. I was studying for an engineering exam once and I needed to ask a question regarding total square feet in an acre. I called him and he instantly blurted out the answer. We had commonality when it came to details and a desire to know facts.

164

My stepmom's Spirit-filled life formed the gateway to my faith. Attending church on Sunday was a must, as were chores. Summers were spent tending to the garden, snipping 5 gallon buckets of beans daily and canning vegetables. She taught me strength and unconditional love. Strict in her parenting, once as a toddler, she put me in my crib for misbehaving and crayons were close by on the dresser, so I proceeded to color my tights. I guess I never liked to be told what to do.

My stepdad is my source of calm and structure. These qualities have helped me to be reasonable and steady throughout my career. He has been a great source of information, as he owns and operates a paving and excavating business. This makes for quick and easy answers when I have a construction question! Together, we have built new roads, installed utilities, and built homes for a development we started in the late 1990's.

Beginning my career in a male dominated engineering realm as a 20 year old female, during the early 1990's, proved to be challenging, frightening and frustrating. It was especially difficult for someone like me to gain respect and cooperation from powerful, successful, politically connected men that didn't trust me and I didn't belong or exist in their world. Ironically, the male engineering bosses I have had throughout my career always encouraged me and pushed me to be more. Through their encouragement, I decided to pursue additional education to obtain more knowledge because, ***Knowledge is power*** and you can't argue facts.

I'll leave you with some of the sayings that I continue to use to get through numerous situations in my life and profession:

- **Pull up your boot straps and keep moving.**
- **Don't get in my sandbox.**
- **If you can't sleep, write it down.**
- **Be a part of the solution and not the problem.**
- **Round to the next dollar and move on.**

Find commonality with others ... *"But in your hearts revere Christ asLord. Always be prepared to give an answer to everyone who asks you to give the reason for the hope that you have. But do this with gentleness and respect'* (King James Edition, 1 Peter 3.15)."

It isn't where you came from, it's where you are going. There will always be challenges and obstacles but the joys of my journey are and will always be my family and career, which motivate me to cross new roads and bridges.

* * *

Lori Kessler
240-409-0707
contractorsolutionsint@gmail.com
www.contractorsolutionsint.com

Marta Brummell

Life Coach, Mom, Wife, Advocate
Owner: Marta Brummell Life Coaching for Young Adults

Marta Brummell

BIOGRAPHY

Marta is a certified Life Coach and Consultant for young adults and their parents. She helps her clients flourish and live authentically by building their confidence from the inside out. The heart of her work isn't about building impressive resumes, but more about cultivating impressive and beautiful humans. She finds these two things to not be mutually exclusive, but both require building a muscle. Marta normalizes the struggle of adolescence and adulthood for both her clients and their parents, and teaches and embodies the tools of patience, self-love, vulnerability, awareness, and intentionality to approach life situations with a restful heart, peace of mind and openness to opportunity.

Marta studied psychology as an undergraduate at the University of Notre Dame, and she received her Masters of Clinical Social Work from the University of Michigan.

After graduate school, Marta became a medical social worker for oncology patients and families at Loyola University Medical Center in Chicago, and then decided to be a stay-at-home Mom for 12 years to raise their four children. Her passion for working with young adults was born when she became an academic advisor at her alma mater, Notre Dame, which led to The Life Coach for her life coaching certification. Marta's coaching is a powerful blend of her advising, counseling, parenting, and mentoring background.

Marta has a thriving private coaching practice and serves as a consultant for parents, high schools, colleges, and universities who are in the business of helping young adults cultivate the necessary life skills to live fulfilling and fabulous lives.

Marta lives in Denver, Colorado with her husband, Craig and their four children.

From Surviving to Thriving

How to Be the Whole Package

by Marta Brummell

"You were born with wings,
why prefer to crawl through life." ~ Rumi

When I was a young girl, my Dad introduced me to the book "The Road Less Traveled". The first line was "Life is hard." The profound nature of those words were lost on me initially, but once I hit young adulthood, I understood what "hard" was. This brand of hard rendered me either simultaneously or singularly broken-hearted, isolated, lost, insecure, and lacking in meaning and purpose. The angst and darkness of those years were disillusioning as I operated from fear, shame, and not feeling good enough. **Thankfully, I learned that there was another way.**

The gift of life coaching came into my world and taught me to question thoughts and belief systems that perpetuated my "hard" narrative. I learned that my unquestioned thoughts and belief systems played a powerful, and ofter destructive, role in creating my reality. I could 'choose' to stay on this crazy train, or shift gears. I chose the latter, and it has made all the difference.

Life coaching is an invitation- a gentle encouragement - to look at your life as it is, here and now, and ask yourself: Where am I not happy? What areas of my life are no longer serving me? What beliefs and thoughts on autopilot do I have about myself that are holding me back from greater well-being and success? What shifts can I make in my mindset and my actions so that I am living from a healthier, kinder, and happier place?

You cannot fully contribute to the world in the way that you are meant to if you do not first concern yourself with your own wellbeing. Cultivating the life skills necessary to flourish in the hard requires a focus inwards. **A kind of soul work.**

As a coach, I help young people answer the question Who Am I? From a place of awareness, presence, curiosity, and compassion which provides the *tools* to shape that growth by first challenging one's own belief systems.

169

"Lauren" sought out my coaching as a freshman in college because she was experiencing anxiety, lack of clarity, sadness, and apathy. She came in as a Biology major, but segued into Industrial Design after realizing that her interests were more in the creative and innovative realm. This shift did not come lightly. Lauren, like so many people, battled aligning her path with her curiosities and strengths instead of basing her choices solely on assumed familial and societal expectations. As Lauren shared, "The question *why* provokes honesty and awareness. In being mindful, you approach things with a curious and peaceful mindset. And by doing so, you can observe which thought structures are debilitating in order to reclaim what thoughts truly feed you. I have never flexed that muscle before - or known it to be part of my mind and heart's anatomy."

As Lauren explored the reasoning for her decision making, she realized that " I had a stubborn protectiveness of my thoughts because I assumed them to be *fact* and held onto them as such." Coaching allowed for "breaking down those walls, and empowering me to refocus thoughts to fuel rather than impede." The greater one's self-awareness, the greater one's ability to change. Living consciously and authentically are key to a sweeter and happier life. Lauren acknowledged that "Living intentionally is a blessing, but it requires repeated engagement and openness to challenging oneself." Our weekly coaching sessions provided a sustained, concentrated and *guided* effort for Lauren to reap the rewards.

My life's work is to help my clients become the whole package: impressive resume, and even more impressive human.

* * *

Marta Brummell
574-286-9052
martabrummell.com
coaching@martabrummell.com

Rhonda Maria Farrah

Author & Founder
Help Me Rhonda Now International, LLC

Rhonda Farrah

BIOGRAPHY

Rhonda Maria Farrah, DRWA, is a visionary and inspirational leader who has spent the past 25 years applying the power and impact of the mind and spirit as crucial in creating personal and professional success - The life we desire - rather than merely living a life of default.

Coach, Author, Speaker, and licensed Art of Feminine Presence™ teacher specializing in LIFEstyle Empowerment, has done consulting work with clients and companies including international Centers for Spiritual Living, and the US Open Wellness Team.

Rhonda authored several books: *The Journey; Inspirations...Thought 4Today... Thought 4 LIFE!;* and completing: *How to Forgive, Live & LOVE ... During the Process of Divorce ... A Journey in Healing & Transformation.*

RHONDA is featured in **America's STAR Entrepreneurs**...an inspirational classic along with some of America's most admired personalities - including Deepak Chopra, Brian Tracy, Joe Vitale, and Denis Waitley.

Rhonda's education and training includes Certification/Member International Coaching Federation. Her professional affiliations include National Association of Entrepreneurs, Women's Entrepreneur Network, and Self-Growth Network. Rhonda has been a Radio Show Host, as well as, expert guest personality, most notably with Voice of America, the largest internet international talk radio network.

Rhonda assists individuals in utilizing their authentic power from within, actualizing their essense & desires. She has demonstrated talent for inspiring and guiding individuals in a positive direction. Her spiritual strength, through a variety of personal & professional life challenges, has enabled her to turn adversity into opportunity.

Rhonda's creative endeavors are dedicated to individual empowerment and the collective conscious evolution of humankind, so we may align perfectly with our Source, fulfilling our purpose while enjoying the process.

Do YOU Have An Olympic Mindset?

by Rhonda Maria Farrah

"Winning is not easy; you always have a tough price to pay, and it doesn't come overnight."

The Olympic Games invite millions of people to watch world-class athletes 'Go for the Gold' in 300 events. Think of the years of discipline, focus, and training to get stronger, faster to shave milliseconds off finish times...truly astounding! Guts and attitude make an Olympic athlete. Our mental attitude develops the incredible inner strength to face the challenges along the way, no matter how we define success.

Attributes of an Olympic Mind Set: Olympic athletes share a mind set that overcomes defeat and moves forward, setting their sights higher than before. And, finally, the realization you compete only with yourself makes us stronger. Trust and Believe... 43 years as a long distance runner...I know! This mind set...the heart set... serves all areas of life...spirit, mind, body, and purpose. On my life's journey, I studied how athletes became Olympians. In my humble, yet, enlightened opinion, it is by cultivating the following mental attitudes.

Will Power: Winning is not easy; you always have a tough price to pay, and it doesn't come overnight. Thinking positively becomes a way of life and naturally leads to dreams and heart desires coming true. A positive attitude bridges the gap between dream and fact with speed and certainty and the added strength to brave and conquer whatever is necessary for still greater achievement.

Determination: When a person is determined one doesn't give up easily in spite of all apparent reasons to quit, knowing if one thing doesn't work, something else will. Reach out with love and risk the rejection we all get from time to time... exercise the determination you have and more will be attracted to you.

173

Motivation: Motivation is the thread that binds our actions into a meaningful synthesized role and gives substance to accomplishing our goals. Once truly motivated, we intuitively know which route to follow. It strengthens our will power and allows nothing to deter us from reaching our desired destination. Others see our example and emulate our attitudes in their own life.

Do the Work: Set goals to excite you, and far away enough to keep busy in their pursuit. Accomplishments have a way of snowballing so each goal, no matter how small, is worth turning into reality. Work hard - and work smart!

Adversity: Trust life and people, knowing that if you are *occasionally* fooled, you are still the winner for you have not lost the capacity to believe. Most of all, strive to maintain the attitude that will continue to serve and protect you from all negative forces that seek to have you lose faith in yourself and your dream.

Focus: Choose to focus on the positive. Think about the way things *can* be done instead of ways they cannot be done. Look to your strengths instead of weaknesses. See possibilities where they didn't exist before. Listen creatively to people who have "done it" and you will pick up new ideas to achieve your goals.

Positive Perspective: Greet each day with gratitude that it is yours. Smile in the face of trivial happenings. Remain calm in times of stress. This way, you attract the people, places and activities as you run the race to claim your highest good!

Let the Games BEGIN!

* * *

Help Me Rhonda Now International, LLC
949-527-1574
rhonda@HelpMeRhondaNow.com
www.HelpMeRhondaNow.com

Geneviève Carle

Certified Business Coach

Master Practicioner
Owner of CGC Services, Inc.

Geneviève Carle

BIOGRAPHY

Geneviève Carle is dedicated to her clients and their business success. Founder of CGC Services Inc., Geneviève specializes in coaching and training executives and their teams to develop all aspects of leadership. Co-Owner and senior partner of Groupe Conseil Larouche & Associates, a firm dedicated to assisting entrepreneurs and corporations to develop business and strategic plans, while assisting in obtaining financial support to bring their projects to fruition.

Geneviève has created a complete ecosystem to address all of her clients' business needs. With more than 25 years of experience in strategic, organizational and operational consulting with high performing leaders, and multi-site multi-disciplinary teams, Geneviève has the training and applied knowledge you seek, in leadership development, process improvement, and change management.

Geneviève is a strong believer in giving back to the community. Certified in Board Management, she supports a number of non-profit organizations. Previously a national leader for one of Canada's top five chartered banks, she is a top performer in most aspects of the business, from Sales to Regulatory Risk Management.

Geneviève is recognized for finding original and deployable solutions to complex problems, in the fields of process automation, standardization and process simplification. As a certified PMP, she delivers solutions on time, on budget, and with unmatched quality.

Geneviève's high energy, passion for new challenges, and strong ability to streamline processes are greatly appreciated. Her gentle people approach allows her to skillfully coach employees and executives alike-equaled only by effectively implementing required changes. Geneviève will be a valued partner for all who desire to lead, and for all who want to improve their performance as leaders.

Top Tips for Top Leaders

The impossible just takes a little longer

by Geneviève Carle

"Whether you think you can or think you can't, you're right." -Henry Ford

The ability to inspire, give direction, and pull people together is crucial to every organization. I am often asked to coach leaders on how to find, build, and cultivate a positive mindset for success! Although each leader has different personalities and challenges, my leaders share one thing in common: *too much to do in too little time.* Curiously, when we analyse their "unfinished business" most tend to not want to relinquish control over the multitude of tasks in their bucket list.

Motivation to not delegate varies from insecurity that no one else can bring the task to its successful conclusion; losing control by handing over responsibility; or feeling irreplaceable to achieve a positive outcome; or simply enjoying the challenge, and wanting to see it through to a successful conclusion.

Many obstacles to delegate may result in undesirable consequences:

- Reduced engagement from top employees, who may lack the confidence to successfully complete assignments.
- Lack of shared thoughts and perspectives.
- Less availability for coaching activities.
- Execution in silos due to limited input from key players leading to sub-par results.
- Other leaders will follow suit and "guard their territory", by not sharing their expertise thereby remaining "indispensable" to the company.
- Increased and undue stress on the leader to produce time-tested principles and ideas.

Leaders as gardeners(helping your team grow)

The following analogy illustrates the dynamics of following Top Tips.

Perennials need to be managed. These great plants provide structure to gardens and flower beds with blooms that return year after year! They do, however, sprawl and may overtake other species if not managed consistently and allowed to grow exponentially. A good gardener manages their perennials, perhaps splitting some to create more space elsewhere to satisfy their need to populate. The same applies to your teams. They thrive while providing structure to your growing business if you provide the right boundaries and opportunities for continued growth.

The concept of companion plants. The use of companion plants is an agricultural technique to increase crop proficiency. Alternatively, some plants have negative impacts on each other, resulting in less than optimal crops. The same applies to team members. Pay careful attention to how you build teams to optimize efficiencies. You want to ensure that teams are diverse in nature, have varied perspectives (which encourages lively discussions), while ensuring teams work most effectively together.

Some people prefer working in the background (shade) while others love the limelight(sunlight). Keep this in mind while determining the environment best suited for individual team members. This applies both to the type of work and projects you assign your team as well as how you reward them. Although it is best to set up a "standardised" reward and recognition program, rewards may differ slightly. For example, when providing an award for someone who loves the limelight, recognition is best announced at a larger team meeting. Alternatively, a more introverted employee would appreciate receiving the award in a more intimate setting, directly with team members, and only a discreet announcement made at the larger meeting of peers.

Roses. Much like the rose, some team members need to be the center of attention. They are durable, beautiful, and produce more than other members. Yet, these same individuals may be prickly and require greater care and attention. Be aware of their sensitive nature and prepare "roses" well before re-planting in a different environment. They may not adapt at first and may take longer to bloom again or - if not handled carefully - may wither on the vine. Do whatever it takes to keep everyone motivated based on their individual personalities. The ability to lead with empathy by looking at things from all different perspectives make the greatest leaders.

Leaders set the tone: Leaders lead by example. The way you delegate and coach your top leaders is how they will emulate your style. Think about the task holistically and don't improvise. What is the end goal? The purpose? The key players? Share their accomplishments to motivate members? What are the key dates and timetables? Allow team members to prepare their own plan of action. Their approach may differ from yours - that's ok. Don't dictate the way it should be done, other than how you do NOT want it done. Follow through with regular updates and coaching sessions by providing support and guidelines. The more success they experience, the more empowered they become, meaning more freedom for you to handle more strategic company positions. **EVERYBODY WINS!**

Manage your schedule by quadrant. Keep a constant eye on your schedule and emphasize important issues vs. urgent tasks to set the tone for your leaders, who in turn, will help their team members do the same. By initiating more strategic and tactical items at a quicker pace, with less interruptions, you create a much more pleasant environment which leads to a more positive outcome for all.

Be careful what and how you measure results.

What gets measured gets managed. Thus, many leaders measure most everything. Sometimes this leads to unintended consequences. People working too quickly may seem productive at first, yet heightened speed may produce a high level of errors, resulting in client dis - satisfaction. Remember that famous

quote: **HASTE MAKES WASTE!** Take time for considerable thought to the measures you implement to truly represent your company's principles and ideals. Look at things from a YES! Perspective

Try to do nothing.

At least make it appear so. This recommendation will bewilder many leaders. However, it is one of the most important tips to follow. **Learn to delegate,** in the right way, at the right time, to the right person. When you do this, you demonstrate to your people that they have earned your trust.

You are **helping them grow.** Be certain to follow through. As they take on new responsibilities, affirm your belief in their worthiness and ability to achieve what they set out to accomplish. This will build their confidence and raise your relationships to a constant state of achieving positive expectations and results.

The impact of change.

Often times, we are so attracted to the benefits of change to our company that we forget that humans are creatures of habit; the true cost of implementation requires changes in behavior. It is very important to understand all impacts of a change before beginning implementation. A change in people's habits are always a challenge, even when they personally made the decision to implement change, let alone when someone else makes the decision for them. Be certain to have quality assurance processes in place. Constant communication and feedback certainly help, but be certain you have a team in place to help with any adjustments required - post implementation.

I shared with you some great tips to make you an even greater leader than you already are. Claim them as your own as you implement them with your leaders and their teams. And, even though the results will certainly be positive for your business, prepare yourself for the huge impact of the positive changes these tips will bring to your team members. **The more you work on the process, the greater your success will be!.**

* * *

Geneviève Carle
info@genevievecarle.com
www.genevievecarle.com
www.gclarouche.com

Laleh Alemzadeh-Hancock

President & CEO
Belapemo & Global Wellness For All

Laleh Alemzadeh-Hancock

BIOGRAPHY

A seasoned executive, life-long entrepreneur, CEO of **Belapemo**, President of **Global Wellness For All**, and conscious parent, Laleh Alemzadeh-Hancock dedicates her career and personal life to inspiring and empowering people to exponentially grow their lives and businesses.

In the last 30 years, Laleh has built top-notch and successful consulting firms, service organizations and product companies. What makes Laleh's leadership and her companies unique is their ability to partner with clients to turn every scenario from "that is impossible" to *"everything is possible"*. The mountain may, at first, appear intimidating; however, once you realize it is not more significant than you, it can be overcome and conquered. The next question will be, "What else is possible that you have not even imagined?"

Laleh has built dynamic teams that specialize in empowering individuals and organizations to increase efficiency and promote growth; to create new divisions or service lines; and to discover overlooked opportunities to create a sustainable culture that values, rewards, and challenges each employee to achieve their maximum potential. Whether Laleh and her teams are partnering with a Fortune 500 company to create $14M in savings, facilitating an entrepreneur around the globe to create a business or increase revenue, or providing tools on greater wellness in their lives, Laleh and her teams are determined to do whatever it takes to empower clients to not only reach, but exceed their desired targets.

An advocate and empowering agent for individuals with special needs or disabilities and their caregivers, Laleh served on the Maryland Governor's Caregivers Support Coordinating Council for four years.

Laleh is an ardent change-agent, **Access Consciousness™ & Joy of Business™ Facilitator**, and a committed benevolent capitalist, with a desire to bring global wellness to the forefront of everyone's awareness. Laleh believes in paying her success forward to the next generation via **Belapemo's Leaders of Tomorrow** program, charitable causes and partnering with the communities where she lives and works.

Being a Leader of Today and for the future.

It all starts with you and your willingness to explore and be curious.

by Laleh Alemzadeh-Hancock

"We have the ability to look at the oneness of all things and how each can contribute to the benefit of the other. This leads to not only empowering other women, but empowerment of all, with no exclusion."

What does it take to be the kind of leader that changes the world and creates a greater future for all? From my perspective, the greatest leaders have a "global wellness" perspective, where the thrival of every element of their lives, of other lives, and of the planet now and the future, are included in their choices.

As leading women, we are in a unique position to lead, nurture and empower from the perspective of global wellness. We have the ability to acknowledge the oneness of all things and how each can contribute to the benefit of the other. This leads to not only empowering other women, but empowerment of all, with no exclusion. Everyone, no matter age, sex, gender, culture, experience or background has something essential and unique to contribute. How we accomplish this begins with being a conscious leader and catalyst for change in our own lives and that of others by remaining always curious, asking questions, and challenging limitations — including the ones that are self-imposed.

One of the greatest challenges women have is learning to include ourselves in the global wellness picture. In the process of creating a greater world - ***do you include you?*** Do you consider your body? Your financial happiness, your instincts, and innate awareness of what is possible in the world?

183

As a leader, you must maximize your ability to include your joy, difference, and brilliance in the big picture. It is not a selfish pursuit - but fundamental elements of leadership, that when applied to your own life, determines how you engage with the world. It also invites others who desire to help create a greater world to play alongside you.

Make you a priority.

Do you consider yourself as much a priority as your job, family or career? While becoming better at prioritizing our wellness, most of us still put everything else first, and our own needs last.

Leadership is being the change we wish to see in the world. When you become a priority in your own life, others will follow your example.

Take time to reflect on how you treat yourself, and ask:

* **Do I treat myself with the same regard I extend to others?**
* **What would it feel like to be treated the way I should be treated?**
* **What can I be or do differently today to make myself a top priority in my life?**

Many of us treat others far better than we treat ourselves. Many of us feel we have never received the regard we deserve. Begin today to change this and make yourself a top priority in life.

Ask for (and be willing to receive) contribution.

Do you believe you have to do everything on your own? How often do you ask for assistance - only when there's a problem?

Asking for contribution is not about being needful or lacking. Contribution empowers you to have more assistance, ideas, and possibilities that maximize your chances of bringing your desires to fruition.

Allowing others to contribute is an important change of mindset that can be developed by asking certain questions. Sample of **Joy of Business™** questions include:

- **Who or what can I add that will be a contribution to what desires are to be created?**

- **Who can I talk to or add that has additional information or can assist in making this greater?**

Whether it's your business or personal life, you can continuously add the contribution of other people, systems, tools and opportunities to reach, and go beyond, your targets.

Nurture your body.

Everywhere you go, your body does too! Are you including its wellbeing? Just as we avoid asking for help unless there's a problem, we have a strong tendency to care for our bodies only when issues arise such as stress, anxiety, injuries or illnesses.

Nurturing your body is fundamental to accessing and experiencing joy, curiosity, ease, and energy that nurtures our lives.

Practice prioritizing your body's wellbeing by taking time every day, to do something to nurture your body. Sample ways to do this include:

- * **Moving your body**
- * **Spending time in nature**
- * **Nurturing touch - a massage, pedicure, or even a hug!**

When you enjoy and nurture your body more, new ideas and inspirations tend to exponentialize.

Trust You.

Do you believe in yourself as a change agent and leader? Or do you believe that you don't have the capacity to make a difference?

Leadership is more than just aquiring the right skills and performing well in your field. Above all, it requires that you trust you and believe it's possible to go beyond where you are now - for your beliefs and points of view determine the choices and actions you will take.

Trusting you allows you to access that which is unique and different about you. Explore ways of trusting you more with these questions:

- What do I know is possible that no one else does?
- What does my business / my life / the earth require of me today?
- Am I willing to trust my instincts and follow them, even if they seem irrational to others?
- Am I willing to listen to expert information, but always choose what I know is best?

Trusting you, your gut-instincts, and innate awareness, will lead you to accomplish more and greater things, whether anyone else believes its possible or not.

Cultivate financial wellness.

Are your attitudes towards creating revenue open and forward-thinking? Limited perspectives about money are plentiful, but so are potential revenue streams. Leaders expand their financial futures by challenging perceived limits, creating financial clarity, educating themselves about money, and seeking possibilities for maximizing revenue. Ask yourself:

- ∗ What is my current income and expenditure?
- ∗ How much revenue must I create per year to have the life I desire?
- ∗ Who or what can I add to maximize my business opportunities and increase revenue streams?
- ∗ Where can I put my money today to create more money now and in the future?

Changing your finances may be necessary in the process of creating financial wellness. Lead yourself forward with curiosity, challenge limited mindsets, and keep asking questions.

Listen to the subtle whispers.

Great leaders are willing to have a vision beyond what is perceived as normal, real or true in the present. They act on what they know is possible, even if it doesn't exist yet.

Expand your mindset beyond the status quo and access the whispers of your knowing with curiosity:

- What else is possible I have not yet considered?
- What can I be or do different today to create greater now and in the future?
- How does it get any better than this?
- What am I capable of that I have never acknowledged?

Creating a greater future isn't about fixing problems or reaching a final destination. It is about listening to the whispers that inspire you to take action beyond pinnacles, barriers or limits.

Leadership for a greater future requires us to embrace the gift in everything and everyone, including ourselves. Challenge limits. Seek greater. Ask questions. Be curious. Value your difference, brilliance, and happiness as you create your life and future. Embody the greatness and kindness you desire to see in the world, and you will become the leading invitation for others to choose their future, too.

* * *

Laleh Alemzadeh-Hancock
President & CEO
www.Belapemo.com
www.globalwellnessforall.com

Kathryn R. Martin

Organizational & Leadership Coach

Kathryn R. Martin

BIOGRAPHY

Kathryn R. Martin, named *'Top Leadership Coach of the Year'* 2018 by the International Association of Top Professionals, coaches non-profit boards, founders and executives to create empowered momentum and leverage moments of change into opportunities for growth, revenue-generation, engagement and meaningful success.

Kathryn's hands-on and intuitive approach reveals a client's purpose, impact and true value, which causes transformational breakthroughs and big shifts. She is known for helping clients at a crossroads quickly get unstuck and create the mindset, language and strategies to move from their 'Point A' into their *extraordinary* 'Point B.'

Kathryn has consulted with over 150 arts and culture organizations, and has supervised, trained and coached professional interim leaders placed in organizations across the United States. Additionally, she has led nine arts and culture organizations through transition as a professional interim Executive Director-most recently serving as interim Executive Director of the Santa Barbara Symphony, Interim President & CEO of the Sharon Lynne Wilson Center for the Arts in Milwaukee, and Executive Director of the Linda Place Foundation in San Antonio.

Before launching her business in 2016, Kathryn served as Vice President at Arts Consulting Group(ACG) for 12 years, Managing Director and SummerFest General Manager at the La Jolla Music Society from 1998 to 2003, and oversaw capital improvement projects and more than 250 events annually as the Production and facilities Manager at the Department of Music, University of California San Diego. Today, Kathryn serves on the Boards of the Association of California Symphony Orchestras and Santa Barbara Symphony.

Helping individuals and organizations have the impact they are meant to have makes Kathryn's heart sing, and she facilitates board and staff visioning summits, is a frequent guest speaker, and works with successful leaders in 1:1 coaching, small group leadership master minds, and in her signature program, the *'Create Your Dream Career (Life!)Impact Intensive'™*.

Love Your Life
Five Lessons for Leaders
by Kathryn R. Martin

> *"Your true value is deeper than the list of skills and accomplishments on your resume. You are more than a job title. You are the impact you have on others."*

I love my life.

The challenges, the moments of vulnerability, the opportunities, the friendships - all of it.

In 2016, I faced a crossroad. I felt a calling to find my voice, do what makes my heart sing, and launch out on my own. The "practical" voices in my head were loud. *What do I have to offer that will make a difference? Will anyone invest in my services? What if I fail?* Even in the face of these fears and uncertainties, I knew I had to take the leap.

It was time.

Looking back, I can say with confidence that the decision to follow that calling has changed my life, and the lives of the women I've had the privilege to coach.

Women are beautifully complex. We are full of power, wisdom, compassion and expertise. We lead and champion important causes. Yet, we can also be unaware of our own value and purpose; creating inadvertent barriers to creating the lives we really want.

Over the past thirty years I've witnessed prominent leaders feel stuck and disillusioned, I'm sharing 5 powerful lessons that have helped both me and my coaching clients reveal their purpose, generate momentum, and curate sustainable and meaningful success in business.

Use joy as your compass.

I had a job that I loved, until I didn't. After 12 years as vice president of a national consulting firm, I was pulled toward creating more meaning in my days. I knew our work had impact, but over time I noticed my frustration. I looked inward, and against the advice of colleagues, I resigned to focus on what made my *heart sing*. This was the first time in my life that I didn't have a concrete plan with strategies to ensure success before making such a large decision. Yet, I took the leap and re-focused my intention from generating business to serving those who I am meant to help.

I became aware that when I "showed up" as my best self, I connected with those who were seeking what I could offer. In the moments where I had the most impact, with the least effort, I felt alive. I felt joy.

I let that guide me and made decisions about services, methodology, fees, schedule and growth - understanding and valuing that when I felt joy, it was a litmus test that I was helping others.

Know your true value.

Your true value is what occurs to others when you show up as your best self. Rather than your job title, salary, education, and accomplishments, your true value is that special thing that you do, in that unique way that you do it. It can feel so natural and effortless, that it can be hard to identify - and we can certainly undervalue it. And yet, it's what sets us apart from everyone else.

It's your noble cause. It's why you are here.

And it's only in knowing it, that you can then make decisions on what to do next, what job will make your heart sing, what salary you should negotiate, what a cover letter should convey, how to network, increase revenue, and more. You'll be able to identify the causes and conditions you need to *nurture* it.

191

Live in the moment. Fully.

My husband was shocked as I said the words to my friend:
"My Son is doing really well, thanks for asking."

"What do you mean?" he said, "He's fighting brain cancer, has dropped out of college and is in constant pain!"

I realized in that moment how much I had grown in the two years since I took the lead into entrepreneurship. I had just spent two hours at my son's bedside as he laughed with the nurses and said that he knew he was going to beat cancer. I was connected, and he was happy.

Living in the moment was a new way of BE-ing for me.

In the beginning, perhaps it was a survival mechanism. With many unknowns and frightening "what if" scenarios, I could only process one moment at a time. However, I began to notice how everything I need is in the present moment.

I seemed to be in the right place at the right time - even as I balanced a thriving new coaching practice with hospital logistics. I adjusted my schedule. My husband and I began watching sunsets. We laughed. We expressed gratitude to those around us, and despite the circumstances, I felt calm.

Test your assumptions about time and money and invest in yourself.

Time and money are tangible and quantifiable resources. We see how much we have and how much we don't. This enables us to make informed decisions. Or does it?

Some of the most transformational moments I've observed happened when it appeared like there wasn't enough time or money for someone to invest in themselves.

TIME: When I was Vice President, I remember a night after working a 10 hour a day and still not accomplishing what was needed. I felt overwhelmed and that it wasn't humanly possible to do it all. Right at that moment, I received an email from an arts leader I respected. She asked for help on a project that was going to have tremendous impact. My heart leaped, and I knew I was going to say yes. In one instant, I had capacity to do more. I made it possible. *But how can this be? Nothing had changed. My calendar was still full.*

MONEY: I remember the first time I faced decision on whether to invest in a year-long leadership mastermind. At first, the decision was straightforward. I couldn't afford it. I remember saying, "This isn't a mindset issue. I'm looking at my bank statement, and I.do.not.have.it." A few hours later, I began thinking a more accurate statement would have been, "I have the money, but I'm choosing to spend it on other things instead." A few more hours later, I realized that if I wanted to achieve the work-life future I envisioned, I needed to take actions that would support that outcome.

In my case, the clear choice emerged that I needed to pursue the beginning of my next chapter. I created a payment schedule, and -while nothing had changed- I had the money.

Choose the words of your vision carefully.

Shortly after marrying, we began trying to get pregnant. It didn't happen. It seemed like every week I was attending another baby shower, and it was hard.

At one of those events, two of the moms attending had created their families through adoption.

I felt a lightning bolt hit me as I realized that my goal was not to get pregnant, it was to be a mom. And, there are lots of ways to be that.

193

Now, as a proud mother of two young adults, my palms sweat just thinking what if I hadn't shifted the word I used to describe what I wanted? Would I have given up in failure?

An invitation:

Reframe your vision and success in terms of impact, set your intention to be your best self (feeling joy) so that you can help others, and then only take the embodied actions (thoughts, feelings, language, actions) that will make that all possible.

Even though I haven't met you yet, I know you are unique. I know there are people, businesses, communities, who are waiting for someone like you to appear. What actions can you take to live fully in your purpose, speak in your authentic voice, "show up" in that way you feel joy and create the ripples of impact that only you can create-and love your life? Your journey begins today.

* * *

Kathryn R. Martin
(858)761-4928 Cell
kathryn@kathrynRmartin.com
www.kathrynRmartin.com

LOVE ♥ LIFE

Life let me love you. You mean everything to me. Let me not take you for granted for there is no replacement for you. Let me always appreciate you, for once you are gone -- you will never return again.

You are the song on my lips, the melody in my heart, the symphony played for me but once. I seek not to explain you, only to love you. Of all the lovers in the world, you are the most constant, the most faithful, the most enduring, and yet the most fickle. For you give the illusion of forever, but forever you cannot stay.

You are a proud lover. You beg not my attention, nor demand it, but merely pass before me in all your splendor, wondering if I will notice you before you must turn and flee. Spill your riches before me. I desire your golden days and hours, more than oil wells or diamond mines.

As I make my way among people, I meet strangers with a smile, and think of the healing power of love. In loving you, I love all of life. Its changes, its moods, and all that comes between. Everything is beautiful because we are together.

You are so important to me that I approach the humblest task with pride and accomplish all that I can. In that way, the market place will respond with pleasure and profits to share with you. I do it all for love of you.

Let me love you. Through all that is and is to be. While the breath of life is warm in my body, while I can still see your beauty and hear you call my name, while I can laugh and make love, shed tears, and be everything you need me to be.

Who else could love you as much as I? Who else could bring me rapture but you? Let us mingle our energies while the glorious sun reclines behind the shadow of the moon, so tomorrow we rise with passion and purpose because we are together again.

© Pat Sampson

Deborah Armstrong

**Owner/Designer of
Deborah Armstrong and Company**

Metal Smith and Jewelry Designer

Deborah Armstrong

BIOGRAPHY

For nearly 30 years, Deborah has been creating exquisite jewelry amassing many loyal collectors including celebrities and dignitaries who seek out her intricately patterned sterling and 18k designs because of their infinite wearability.

At the University of Colorado, Deborah majored in art and art history. After moving to Los Angeles, her first jobs were costume and wardrobe for TV programs including *All in the Family*. This, along with her sculpting background, provided the experience necessary to become a model-maker for George Lucas' *Industrial Light and Magic* special effects firm and later, *Apogee*. With her interest in television and film piqued, Deborah moved from a career in model-making to film editing.

After marrying Jon Connolly, Deborah moved to New York City. Since film editing was union controlled, her work on the west coast was not recognized on the east coast so Deborah had to re-invent herself. She began a career in advertising where she worked for DDB Needham on such diverse accounts as Clairol, Volkswagen, Mobil Oil and Amtrak. But her artistic urges weren't being met.

In the late 1980s, Deborah returned to her creative roots and started taking jewelry classes. **She was classically trained at Cecelia Bauer's studio in NYC where she applied techniques used by the ancient Greeks. At Parson's, she learned wax carving and how to make molds so she could duplicate her unique designs.**

She launched her company in 1996 and from the very beginning, she developed a devoted following. Her jewelry has been featured in many top fashion magazines and is now worn by celebrities including Halle Berry, Jennifer Connelly, Faith Hill, Heidi Klum, Diane Sawyer, Diane Von Furstenberg, Sharon Stone and Vanessa Williams. She is even on the Supreme Court as worn by Justice Sonia Sotomayor.

The Big Leap

by Deborah Armstrong

"The artist never entirely knows - We guess. We may be wrong, but we take leap after leap in the dark." ~Agnes de Mille

The key to creativity is risk taking.

How can you make anything unique without taking a leap of faith? As Henri Matisse once said, *"Creativity takes courage."*

When I was at Parsons, I met a fellow student. Both of us were floundering, trying to figure out how to apply what we were learning into something meaningful. She chose to go for her MFA. I jumped in with both feet and started doing trade shows with zero experience, just a passion for creating jewelry.

If I had methodically amassed the information necessary to launch a business, I would have been so daunted that I never would have taken a step. In those years, my learning curve was perpendicular. Obstacles were a daily occurrence and I just had to figure them out and move on. It required being flexible, accepting ambiguity or the unpredictable, making connections between seemingly unrelated phenomena and then finding solutions.

Creativity involves two processes: thinking, then producing.

If you have ideas but don't act them, you are imaginative, not creative. The thinking part requires feeding your mind and your soul. So drink in art, poetry, literature, nature, dance, music, film, every type of stimulation that will fire up your creativity. If you can remember what completely absorbed you as a child, you may have a clue as to your passion.

The producing part means hunkering down, never giving up, exploring alternate solutions with no fear of failure. Edison said, *"I have not failed a thousand times. I have successfully found a thousand ways to not make a light bulb."* Of his countless mistakes, 1,093 of them became patents. In his case, the process became the solutions. Through it all he never stopped experimenting and asking questions. So ask questions, at the very least it will make life more interesting and ultimately, more fulfilling.

Connect the Dots.

"Creativity is intelligence having fun." ~Albert Einstein

Another part of creativity is the art of making connections. When you open your eyes to this way of thinking, everything around you becomes fair game. The books you read, the music you listen to, and the people who surround you can all contribute. Ideas begin to co-mingle with one another, percolate and soon you have created something entirely new.

Travel, in particular, inspires me. Photos I took of the intricate tile work in the Alhambra Palace in Granada later became one of my best selling collections.

Ask any creative when they are in their "zone", they feel positive and have greater energy and far less likely to experience boredom. You don't succeed because you are destined; **you succeed because you are determined.**

I worked on one design for months. It involved alternating two different sized triangles. Every time I cast the pieces and then assembled them, it became an unwearable spiral no matter how I changed the dimensions.

Eventually, I separated the two elements, integrated pearls and used each in a different necklace. These two designs were featured in bridal magazines and walked down many an aisle. Had I been a better geometry student, I would have figured it out much earlier.

Failure IS an Option

"Do what you feel in your heart to be right, for you'll be criticized anyway." ~ Eleanor Roosevelt

You have to accept the fact that sometimes your audience just won't get what you do.

Every great work has had its share of critics. F. Scott Fitzgerald had 122 rejection slips before he sold a story. But when someone discovers your work, it builds confidence and with confidence comes new work. So while the critics knock you around, make more art. Sure everyone wants to be liked, but part of being a creative artist is learning how to take a hit, picking yourself up and doing it again.

One of my clients is a store in Canada. For years, I would see her at trade shows and she would ask countless questions, probing me about my process and where I thought the trends and market were going. I discovered early on that I cannot follow a trend. I have to stick with what moves me.

Days after the show she would call with a substantial order then, just before shipping, she would cancel. It became a running joke in the studio. I knew she carried several lines that were upper end and was discouraged that she was so uncertain about me. Finally, I offered to do a trunk show to prove her clients would respond. A dozen years later, I remain one of her steadfast designers.

Obviously, everyone isn't going to like your work. So you have to put yourself on the front line and go out and find the ones that do. That's the hard part. There is no road map. If it were easy, everyone would do it. Lots of people make art, a tiny fraction actually sell it and make a living. Once you find your audience, you build a following and fuel it with fresh material.

So instead of protecting your work or running away from criticism, you need to take pride in the fact that you can handle the critics. You should embrace the fact that maybe you are wired a little differently and you're not afraid to be an outsider. You need to understand that even though you may not always succeed you're not going to stop trying because someone doesn't like what you do. Remember, it is never going to get easier, you just get stronger.

* * *

Deborah Armstrong
203-253-3506
deboraharmstrongandcompany@gmail.com
www.deboraharmstrong.com

T I M E

If you awaken one morning to find on your doorstep a treasure chest brimming with sparkling diamond, rubies, and pearls, what would you do? Would you scatter the contents up and down the sidewalk to be trampled? Would you give away your treasure indiscriminately? Or appreciate your newly aquired fortune and determine how to put it to its best use?

Each morning you are presented with a fortune greater than diamonds -- a treasure sparkling new, and irreplaceable. Do you greet your gift with a dull yawn of boredom, hardly noticing the riches that await? Or do you trade your wealth of golden days and hours, only for something of value?

Time is your most valuable possession. You need time to dream, to plan, to work. Time to set goals and reach them; time to learn, to grow, to face challenges, to overcome obstacles. As you go about your day, focus your attention on the present moment. The past may hold lessons and the future promise, but only the present offers the opportunity to act.

You would not trade your most valuable diamond for a synthetic stone, no matter how brightly it shone, because you would be exchanging items of unequal value. And how about spending time wishing you had more money when you could be earning it - or using a large block of time for five small disjointed projects instead of that one big project you've been meaning to get under way? Save rainy day projects for rainy days and make use of the sunlight while it is yours.

The treasure chest of time is open before you. What will you do with the days, months, and years ahead? Will you look back when the sun begins to set, as it will, knowing your treasure was exchanged for the best of which you were capable?

Lancia Soans

Owner: LANCIA DESIGNS

Entrepreneur, Artist and Designer

Lancia Soans

BIOGRAPHY

Lancia has made it her life mission to help those looking to reclaim the art of communication in the digital world. Inspired at a tender age by parents who were the epitome of style, and design(her mother a designer of handbags, and embroidery, and her father gifted with impeccable style and grace) and who communicated through letters, cards and gifts, instilled in her a deep sense of warmth and appreciation in relationships.

With her innate flair for Fashion, and Design, and through her extensive international travel, Lancia sought Modern architecture as her palette for developing her own artistic style and design to create beauty in the world.

Lancia owns and operates a boutique Art and Design company, Lancia Designs. As a curator and creator of *A Polished Lifestyle,* Lancia creates stunning polished pieces of art on metal and glass. In her pursuit of relentless creativity, she finds novel ways of capturing her love for modern architecture; creating exquisite polished Gift Boxes, and luxurious Invitations and Stationery. A firm and ardent believer in the *Art of Appreciation,* she creates one of a kind Thank You Cards, and Note Cards that leave an indelible impression, strengthening her relationships with her partners, friends and families.

Lancia was born and raised in Bombay (of Portuguese heritage), attended Little Flower of Jesus High School, and graduated from the University of Bombay with a major in Sociology. She later moved to the U.S., and attended Florida Atlantic University, studying Communication and Journalism, and returned to Bombay and married her college friend she knew for ten years. Together they moved to New Zealand, and later to Canada. Recognizing her gift for style and Design, she attended the International Academy of Design in Toronto, and majored in Multimedia Design, starting her career developing online simulation programs for Microsoft Office. She now lives with her husband in Virginia.

Art-A Gift that Refreshes the Soul

What Makes Art Therapeutic

by Lancia Soans

> *"Art washes away from the soul the dust of everyday life"* - Pablo Picasso

How does one find inspiration in the mundane activities of life? How do you find your way amidst the fragments of dreams and desires? These are questions each of us thinks about as we navigate our space in the world. Here are some ways we are able to recognize the therapeutic resonance of art.

When we lift our eyes to heaven, or we find inspiration in nature that is never hurried, but harrowed in season. When we find moments of wonder in a sunset, or a sunrise, painted by the Greatest Artist who lives eternally. We remember that we are His creation made in His likeness.

When we are given opportunities to look at those we encounter even in the brief moments of our life through the eyes of our maker, we realize that we are like walking pieces of art in all our varied hues.

We are all artists on this planet set free to paint our strokes on the hearts we meet at different stages in our lives.

What we become rests on the strokes that lift us in the bleakest moments of our life.

The lines that draw us and the lines that move us, create the lines that shape us.

Why is Art a Personal Sanctuary?

As an artist and designer of modern art, I am often asked the question, what is the inspiration behind my art. I believe every artist goes through a metamorphosis of the soul at a deeper level that can be experienced at the moment of creation of a work of art. It has been birthed a million times over through our perceived

205

or actualized imagination, through our relationship with people and things, and through the opening of hearts and minds to receiving that what we do not yet see.

Some see meaning with intention before the brush dips into the palette, others let it just be. Kathleen Denis a wonderful painter whose work I admire very much once stated that she likes to think that *'God lets her hold the brush.'* The next time you start to draw or paint, know that you are always sharing that special part of you. My thought has been *'color your own lines and you will color a rainbow.'* Think of the time you see a rainbow in the sky, how does it make you feel; elated, joyful, filled with wonder? This is why art is personal, it is your experience.

Why is Art a Legacy of Motion and Innovation?

Artists are in motion, and their art is an extension of this ephemeral movement, communicating thoughts and emotions in the most lucid and sinuous form; *World of Dance* showcases this movement of art in motion. Fusion of lyrics, and of music like in the song *What a Wonderful World*, a remake (of the original sung by Louis Armstrong) now created with a blend of *Somewhere Over the Rainbow* (originally sung by Judy Garland) and sung by Israel shows us that Art is innovative and in motion; new ideas bursting through old opuses. The morphing and layering of voices, lyrics and notes in music create a harmony and expression of myriad souls expressing ethos of one but in a congruence of many. You will experience this in your own life as you stand in the solitude of your gift transient only to the growth of your being.

* * *

Lancia Soans
info@lanciadesigns.com
703-944-5508
www.lanciadesigns.com

Shelley Joy

Internationally Acclaimed

Fine Art Artist

Shelley Joy

BIOGRAPHY

Shelley Joy is a uniquely spiritual American artist who from her early years was touched by the unity of color in nature as it applies to the duality of purpose in the human condition - both comic and tragic - in God's creation.

Her interests and influences are not simply in the USA. At age 15 she held her first exhibition at the historic *Museo de San Miguel de Allende* in Mexico continued her studies in Greece at the Aegina Arts Center.

A native of Boston, Massachusetts, she moved to New York City in 1978 to pursue her artistic vision in acting, comedy, dance, music and painting. She received formal studio training at the Boston Museum School of Fine Arts and the Arts Students League in New York.

Shelley believes that to become an artist you sign up on the imagin--ary dotted line for life. You venture your heart, soul and spirit with the knowledge that success can come only with the experience that trial and error bring. Her awareness of comedy, music and the theatre give her paintings the sense of the dramatic and mysterious. Whether observing her *Mountain Series* or her *modern abstractions,* the viewer perceives evidence of a deep empathy for the texture of sensuality in nature and the sensitivity of character in the human frame.

Seeking the turning point of abstraction out of figuration, Shelley has exhibited at group shows with David Bowie, Jerry Garcia and Ron Wood at Ambassador Gallery and Jean Paul Basquiat in New York, the Vanderbilt Museum, Long Island, NY, the Toyamaya Museum, Japan, and the New Atrium Museum of the Louvre in France, among many more.

Shelley was honored for her contributions in fine art. As an Artist in Times Square building, New York, June 21 2018 through Marquis Who's Who.

The Color of Faith in Art and Art in Faith.

Soul and Spirit Beyond the Virtual in the politics of Felt Experience

by Shelley Joy

"We swim in a sea of digital ubiquity but how as citizens and artists can we truly benefit from the tsunami of ideas, information and image in the new digital era, fake or real?"

I believe that to become an artist particularly a painter is a life-time commitment and osmosis. You sign up on the imaginary dotted line for life with your heart, faith, soul and spirit - and you keep to your code of painting daily, weekly, yearly. Artistic evolution evolves for a reason.

When I was a teenager I had the audacity and ambition to be a good painter. But it is the knowledge that comes with trial and error that makes you honest and humble. Over and over again before you develop - and keep developing - before the accomp--lished hand of an artist truly manifests.

Human beings, I feel, are instinctively attracted to COLOR whether they realize this innate attraction or not - we are born into a world of primeval color and charms of nature, space, movement, time and light. Nature explodes with color in the world. So, by my own appreciation of nature, color is the true manifestation and harmolodics of light and shapes and being and form combined.

Today, I paint as an abstract colorist by preference Schopenhauer said "All art aspires to the condition of music" - he must have had Bach and Beethoven in mind - meaning all art aspires towards the condition of abstraction and I would add in painting toward the condition of hue, of shades, of color. However, to learn to appreciate color and palette for landscapes based on the Parisian and The Hudson River school of landscape art - primarily to learn about atmosphere and color values, this theory of color also involves science. It is important to me to paint from the "MODEL" from the human form.

In my early days in stand-up comedy, and everything you see about us today, you cannot take yourself or the maelstrom too seriously. Yet we must believe that seriousness comes from empathy and humility and not the absurdity of ego or bragadaccio. Paradoxically, my paintings have become serious and devoid of humor. It's the intense aggravation and situations of life, while trying to create and live, where humor is born and melts into seriousness.

People in it of themselves are fun and funny when not perhaps terrifying. I am attached to a philosophy to uplift people, in part due to unmitigated sadness and irony reflecting about the world. I always keeps optimistic and a positive spirit in the way circum--stances look above and through the sky and over the horizon.

The Art of Commerce and Digital Commerce

In art you have to work just as hard whether you have the prospect of selling a painting or not - so you have to keep on working - perfecting and going into the unknown zone - especially if your work is abstract because of the element of surprise with active color interaction. The goal is to just get better and give the painting the best you have to offer and don't be afraid of mistakes even if it means losing your time and energy.

Commerce and selling paintings can be exhilarating when people appreciate your work and you know it will enhance their home or workspace. Once you have a value on your work, you really own a 'property' that you're trying to sell. Time, money and aesthetic value from your artistic expression is pleasing. But where do we put digital in art today and art in digital?

My philosophy is fundamentally based in the existence. I believe God watches and lives inside us. We have to be as humble and honest as possible for God's respite and respect. Have a heart of thankfulness, gratitude, even when things fall apart and look beyond repair and so, so unfair. **Beyond circumstances beyond control, love is the first truth amid harsh realities.** Give as much as you can. Philanthropy is important - when you're in the wilderness try to find peace within the scary unknown because you will come through and the answers will come and you will abound.

Consider small success's just as much as larger success so it becomes a habit, when you're filled with love and joy remember it. Because in life it may dissipate and that feeling will sometimes diminish. But, LOVE is the most essential gift a human being can have.

Sometimes walking in the unknown is ok - you can laugh and cry and find glimpses of the essence of yourself. Sometimes, it's good to collaborate with other women because art is still a male dominated world and it takes stamina and physical strength to go forward together.

Walk with people from all walks of life. Set goals for your imagination - dance, create, play or be around music masters. Theater is the portrait of mankind. So it's a good mirror. ThinkBig, wealth isn't always evil, Think tanks and wealth can move forward across the globe to eradicate health problems and educate and advance fellow human beings.

I wish everyone love, peace, and joy, in color.

Namaste.

* * *

Shelley Joy, Fine Arts Painter
www.shelleyjoy.net
shelleyjoy12@icloud.com
shelleyjoy12@gmail.com

FAITH

Faith is the all-important key to unlock the door of endless possibilities. Faith is a forward movement. The mind of faith does not toy too long with methods and techniques and refuses to consider alternatives. It vividly pictures the results, takes the first step, and knows with unshakeable certainty that those results will follow.

Faith is action. A dependency upon facts, figures, and circumstances is not faith; it is braver than that. An investment in the capabilities of others is not faith; faith is freer than that. Moving along a well-traveled route to a sure destination, with safe passage guaranteed is not faith; faith is more adventuresome than that. Faith is a person's advancement into the unknown armed only with a dream and the belief in one's own ability to make that dream come true.

Faith is the quality that makes human equality true. People may be separated by sociological barriers or by differences imposed by circumstances subject to birth and environment, but to each person is granted the ability to believe in oneself to the exact measure needed to lift one beyond circumstances to a beautiful reality of one's inner being. It is this kind of faith that transforms apparent mental and physical limitations into learning centers for the soul.

Faith is proof of its own existence. If there were no magic in the power of believing, people would soon stop believing. But we don't. We go on in the face of unbelievable obstacles and over-whelming odds. There is truth to the magic that the power of believing is available to everyone universally and indiscriminately, and that keeping the faith will transform circumstances beyond physical explanation.

Eileen DiFrancesco, M.D.

Psychiatrist, Psychopharmacologist

Diplomate of the American Board
of Psychiatry and Neurology

Eileen DiFrancesco, M.D.

BIOGRAPHY

Dr. DiFrancesco opened her private practice over 20 years ago. Straight out of residency she was recruited to a private research center using Quantitative Electroencephalography, QEEG to diagnose and treat individuals with Attention Deficit Disorders, Obsessive Compulsive Disorders and Learning Disabilities.

She then returned to Mount Sinai where she worked with hospitalized patients suffering with Schizophrenia, Bipolar disorder, Depression, Addiction and other conditions requiring inpatient treatment. In addition she was involved in Neuroimaging Research looking at new onset Schizophrenia. Her skills were used to diagnose and determine which patients would be likely to later develop Schizophrenia based on new onset Psychotic symptoms.

She believes assessment of genetic and environmental contributions to symptom presentations must be thorough as this is the first step to determine treatment. She also held concurrent appointments at Rockefeller University, Cornell and New York Hospital working both in clinical and research roles in the treatment of Addictive diseases.

Dr. DiFrancesco worked at the Fountain House in Community Psychiatry where she treated homeless mentally ill. She was involved in helping them transition from homelessness and providing medication for their symptoms. Fountain House is nationally known for its treatment model and excellence in caring for homeless mentally ill individuals.

Dr. DiFrancesco graduated with honors from the University of Pennsylvania where she received her bachelor's degree. After receiving her medical degree from Temple University School of Medicine, she received additional training from both Psychiatry and Neurology residencies, she completed her residency training in psychiatry at the Mount Sinai Medical center in New York City.

Dr. DiFrancesco is Board Certified as a Diplomate of the American Board of Psychiatry and Neurology. She was in first class of Psychiatrists required to complete recertification every 10 years in order to keep up with the growing body of clinical and Neuroscience advances. She was recertified again in 2007 and again in 2017.

Beyond Nature and Nurture is Choice

by Eileen DiFrancesco, M.D.

"One of our greatest gifts is that of potential, recognizing and fulfilling it provides meaning to our lives."

Choosing Peace of Mind

Witnessing my brother's seizures at an early age had a strong psychological impact on me. My desire to help others and the recognition that I was highly sensitive to the suffering of others started here.

The medical professionals recommended institutionalization and stated he would not progress mentally beyond the age of a five-year-old. He was not institutionalized and eventually graduated from high school and has been steadily employed and able to care for himself. It was extremely upsetting that my brother could have been treated that way and I wanted to know what the doctors knew and didn't know that made their recommendations so wrong.

I was fortunate to have the opportunity to study Psychology at the University of Pennsylvania, where my focus was on Physiological Psychology. Understanding the biological underpinnings of thought, emotion and behavior was my goal and would shape the course of my education from this point through completion of my residency. I was determined to learn as much as possible about the brain, what it does and what I could do about it.

What I took away from my education was the knowledge that nature provides a genetic predisposition and that every significant experience after birth contributes to the development of our perceptions. I was confident from my training that I had learned from some of the best teachers in Psychology, Psychiatry and Neurology. I felt ready to use my skills to help others. My clinical experience ranges from treating patients with Schizophrenia, Bipolar disorder, Depression, Addiction, ADHD, OCD and others. It is an exciting time to practice Psychiatry.

My goal in working with patients is to understand their unique needs and meet them. There is no single pill or therapy that suits all patients. At times their genetic predisposition dominates as the source of their suffering and other times their background and development environment cause habitual ways of experiencing life that creates suffering. It is critical to take the time to make this assessment. My treatment approach ranges from medication to meditation.

I believe that a healthy brain is key for wellbeing, balance and optimal functioning. Ultimately, helping others see what their potential is and figuring out how to use it is my goal. Everyone has a right to happiness and peace of mind.

* * *

Eileen DiFrancesco, M.D.
(917)699-7845
http://difrancescopsychiatry.com/
md@doctord.nyc

Mary Clement, N.D.

Naturopathic, Homeopathic Physician

Mary L. Clement

BIOGRAPHY

Dr. Mary Clement, a licensed naturopathic physician, has practiced natural medicine and homeopathy in Gig Harbor, Washington, since 1991.

Before attending medical school, Dr. Clement graduated from the University of Texas in 1973 with a BFA, after which she spent many years in the garment industry as a buyer for a large department store, a merchandise manager for a children's division of a sportswear company, and a designer and manufacturer of women's apparel and outerwear. She and her business partner received a special Governor's award for opening the first private industry, a garment manufacturing plant, in the Purdy Women's State Prison in Washington State.

At the age of 36, she left the "rag" clothing business to enroll at Bastyr University, an accredited naturopathic medical school in Seattle, Washington. She graduated with a Doctorate in Natural Medicine at the age of 40 years old and then went on to earn her RN degree as a compliment to her naturopathic medical knowledge.

In Dr. Clement's practice, her most effective modalities include homeopathy, kinesiology (Muscle Response Testing or MRT), NAET, Neuro-Emotional Technique(NET), Cranial Sacral and Reiki.

Through the practice of energy medicine and the use of applied kinesiology, Dr. Clement developed her intuitive skills, which facilitate her intuitive "angel" readings. In 2003, Dr. Clement attended Doreen Virtue's Angel Therapy Training in California. The ATP training provided her with confidence to provide channeled readings for over fifteen years.

After 27 years practicing energy medicine, Dr. Clement practices part-time and devotes more of her time to her treasured hobbies, including throwing pots on the wheel and acrylic painting. She also loves to travel, hike and cycle with her daughters and her friends. Dr. Clement has two beautiful grown daughters, the younger, a teacher, and the elder, a medical doctor. She feels truly blessed.

I LOVE HOMEOPATHY

Homeopathy creates miracles.

by Mary Clement, RN, ND

"The highest ideal of cure is the speedy, gentle, and enduring restoration of health by the most trustworthy and least harmful way."
Samuel Hahnemann, Founder of Homeopathy

When I was introduced to homeopathy in naturopathic medical school, I was skeptical of this unconventional healing modality and I just could not comprehend that dissolving sugar pellets under my tongue, was credible medicine at all. To graduate, I was required to take an introductory homeopathy class, so I attended with great curiosity.

It wasn't long into the course that my head was spinning while memorizing all the unusual names of the remedies; Nux vomica, Lycopodium, Arnica, Passiflora, Staphisagria. What was even more confusing to me were homeopathy's strange concepts, particularly the concept of a homeopathic remedy being more powerful the more diluted down it was from the original substance.

When "homeopathic prescribing" was described as a "spiritual" experience by a fellow clinician, I felt numb to her experience. As a second year student who was struggling to stay on top of an intense curriculum, I felt overwhelmed and mentally exhausted, void of her passion. Years would pass before I readily embraced my new role as a spiritually directed, homeopathic physician.

What is Homeopathy? A Brief Background.

Homeopathy was intuited and created by Samuel Hahnemann in the late 1700's in Germany as a rebellion against bloodletting, leaching and administering mercury until the patient finally gave up life.

Homeopathic remedies are made mainly from minerals, animal substances and plants and go through a process called potentialization. The more dilute, the greater the cellular, energetic reaction in the body thereby, the more powerful. A remedy that is diluted 200 times from the original substance is more powerful that the same remedy that is diluted only 30 times.

In Europe, homeopathy became so important and popular that it soon spread to America. At the turn of the 20th century, there were around 300 homeopathic hospitals, scores of homeopathic colleges, tens of thousands of homeopathic practitioners in the US.

In 1900, $4000 was granted by Congress to commission the American Institute of Homeopathy to erect an impressive monument in Hahnemann's honor near Scott Circle in Washington, DC. The monument, which was erected during a White House national ceremony in June of 1900, was a symbol of the impact that Hahnemann's contribution made to medicine and to health of our nation.

The large bronze statue of Hahnemann is seated on a pedestal, underneath which is inscribed in Latin, "As Like Cures Like." Four large curved panels behind the statue depict his life as a learned student, a respected chemist, a devoted teacher, and a caring physician. This statue demonstrates the importance and acceptance of homeopathy in the United States at the turn of the 20th century.

The Main Concept - The Law of Similars.

Homeopathy is based on the Law of Similars, meaning that "like cures like". Homeopathy stimulates a person's innate ability to heal and can treat both acute and chronic conditions without side effects. Homeopathy does not interfere with other treatments or with drugs and homeopathy is safe for all ages, from infants to our elders.

Miracles, miracles, miracles!

I have seen more miracles in my practice with homeopathy than with any other healing modality. Now I live and love the concepts of homeopathy. I have seen homeopathy help depression, anxiety, insomnia, arthritis, herpes, alopecia, eczema, psoriasis, fatigue, fibromyalgia, menstrual difficulties, hormone imbalances and so much more....

Some of my favorite remedies:

Nux vomica. This remedy is commonly prescribed for the person who tends to be Type A, overworked, drinks tons of coffee to keep going, sometimes indulges in too much alcohol, and who can be very impatient. They tend to wake up around 3-4am thinking about projects and all they have to do the next day. This person may have gastric ulcers, heartburn, digestive complaints or headaches.

Coffea cruda. This is another remedy from the ill effects of too much coffee or the symptoms like a person has had too much coffee; jittery, nervous, insomnia. This is a great sleep remedy when one's mind won't turn off, like when one has too much coffee

Passiflora incarnate. Another great sleep remedy for the person who needs to relax at bedtime.

Arnica montana. Well-known remedy for bruising and soreness. May be for any condition where the muscles or body feels bruised, such as after a hard workout, or working out in the yard all day.

Lycopodium clavatum. Great remedy to build confidence. This remedy can be for someone shy or insecure or for someone who is a bully because he/she is insecure. The person tends to have digestive complaints and may have eating disorders.

Baryta carbonica. The person who would benefit from this remedy is immature or childish. Has annoying behavior. Seems young for the age. Great for all ages, even adults who just seem to never grow up, or for kids who do not want to grow up!

Silica. This remedy is for anyone who gets sick frequently, who has low resistance to infections. Particularly good to take during the cold and flu season as prevention. Silica helps the body's immune response and defenses.

There are around 20 main remedies called **polycrests**, and at least 5,000 other homeopathic remedies. I firmly believe that every person should be familiar with the healing properties of homeopathic medicine and should have basic remedies in their medicine cabinet. In fact, both of my daughters went off to college with their own homeopathic kits.

My self-paced online comprehensive course in homeopathy.

With my love of and passion for homeopathy, I have developed an online course in homeopathy. This self-paced, online course provides invaluable information on remedies for acute and chronic conditions as well as remedies for emotional concerns. You will have access to the information for one year.

My 4-Week Webinar on the basics of homeopathy.

In addition to the online, self-paced, course in homeopathy, I also teach a personalized 4-week webinar series on basic and also advanced homeopathic remedies. These courses are designed to give a person proficient tools in a short period of time to be able to use homeopathic remedies effectively.

To learn more about my Homeopathic courses, please contact me directly. I look forward to sharing my information with you. Thank you.

* * *

Dr. Mary Clement
maryclementnd@gmail.com
www.drmaryclement.com
www.spiritofhomeopathy.com

Dr. Alison Parker Henderson

Holistic Chiropractor
Miracle Wellness Center

Dr. Alison Parker Henderson

BIOGRAPHY

Dr. Alison Parker Henderson, a Washington, D.C. chiropractor with nearly 25 years of experience, has had an extraordinary career in health care. Her journey eventually took her on a mission to Ghana, Africa, and she uses her African indigenous experience to help improve the health of US citizens.

Dr. Parker dreamt of being a doctor since a child. While studying pre-medicine at Howard University, she joined the school's Taekwondo Team and earned a Black Belt; and qualified for the 1988 USA Olympic team. An unfortunate neck injury disqualified her final competition. But as fate would have it, the chiropractor at the US Olympic Training Center, encouraged her to pursue a career in Chiropractic.

Dr. Parker has practiced as a Holistic Chiropractor in Washington, D.C since 1995. Focusing on improving the health of her community, she participated in health fairs with government agencies, churches and other community projects. She was co-host on radio shows in DC including WPFW's Joni Eisenburg, Heal DC, and Jay Winter Night-wolf, Improving Native American Lives, Kathy Hughes, WOL radio, with Brother Bey's Health Talk Radio and other local TV and radio projects aimed at improving health of low income residents.

In Ghana, Dr. Parker helped to teach and provide chiropractic care and natural health to the citizens of Kumasi and Accra. She assisted Archbishop of Ghana, Archbishop Duncan Williams of Action Chapel, in opening and managing a new integrated health clinic. She is currently a co-partner of Paradigm Health Center in Accra, with Dr. Grisel Industrioso.

Her awards include Department of Navy Certificate of Commenda-tions, National Phlebotomy Association, Phlebotomist of the Year, D.C. General Hospital, US National Taekwondo 1986 Gold medalist and 1988 US Olympic Team trial competitor Top 3 Women's Welter Weight, Defense Logistics Agency, Certificate of Appreciation Health Program, Charter Health Certificate of Appreciation, S.O.M.E Caregivers program Award.

Dr. Alison Parker Henderson

The Miracles of Chiropractic
Helping others nourishes the soul
...and leads to enlightenment.
by Dr. Alison Parker Henderson

"The doctor of the future will give no medicine, but will interest his patient in the care of the human frame, in diet and in the cause and prevention of disease" ~Thomas Edison

As a caring holistic chiropractor, practicing in Washington, D.C., I have to state my feelings. How appalled I am at the current state of health care in the USA. Although U.S.A. health care system is much more sophisticated than in Ghana, many U.S citizens can't afford health insurance. Health care for African-American people in our country is sometimes worse than for my Ghanaian patients who have very little money.

Health care is one of America's biggest and most profitable industries. A health care system maximizing profits based on sick care, instead of keeping people healthy by providing preventive medical procedures. Health insurance premiums are too high for middle class people to keep maximum profits is a shame. Health care is the right of all individuals in a society and should be available and affordable to all equally. (9th Amendment).

As an individual, and a chiropractor/healer, I always provide services even though people may not have the means to pay. Many people including children are falling through the cracks. Chiropractic is a preventive medicine, the art and science of manipulation for maximum nerve flow throughout the body. There are many chiropractic mission trips throughout the world saving lives. Chiropractors see miracles everyday because we allow the body to heal itself.

In traveling to Africa, India and other countries, including Peru, I see vast poverty amongst lush surroundings. I have witnessed miracles, just through the art of chiropractic alone, with "barren" women having babies, and incurable diseases cured or greatly improved. The cost was minimal.

I worked in Kumasi, Ghana for over a year, teaching people how to take care of themselves and helping improve sanitation habits so that women would have healthier babies. Next, I moved to Accra. I began working with the Archbishop of a Ghanaian church. Together we built a clinic in the church compound and started a program integrating traditional African and western medicine. ***Working in Africa is a humbling experience and I am grateful for the opportunity to help others.***

Every year on the anniversary of the grand opening of the church clinic, I go back to Ghana to bring clothes and toys for children I sponsor there. I bring medical supplies for the clinic, Yet, surprisingly, the state of health care for African-American people is sometimes worse than for my Ghanaian patients who have no money. I am developing a non-profit health clinic to help people in the USA who do not have insurance, get health screenings and find resources to improve their health and quality of life.

We have enough resources on this planet that not one single person need go hungry or lack access quality health care. ***It's called sharing.*** The rise in vegetarianism is a hopeful promise to save the planet as we consider not killing animals for food. Racism and hate are out-dated. Love is the answer to a brighter future for the human race. Our children and even the animals show us this everyday. Compassion. Only peace and love will heal our planet and bring happiness and unity to our world. No U.S. citizen should be without access to proper healthcare. We must all love and help one another. I pray that the generations coming will have universal free health care for all.

* * *

Dr. Alison Parker Henderson
Miracle Wellness Center
202-288-8354
Doctorfaith11@icloud.com

Maria Horstmann

Founder, Owner

Be Fab - Be You, LLC

Maria Horstmann

BIOGRAPHY

Maria Horstmann, MBA, CPT, PNL1, **Transformational Speaker, Health and Fitness Coach**, and **Corporate Wellness Consultant**, is a phenominal example of someone who had the courage to leave the security of the corporate world. In 2014, to follow her passion of empowering busy professionals and go-getters to lose weight, boost energy and confidence, and build physical and mental strength.

Maria once had prediabetes and struggled with chronic digestive and gastrointestinal issues. She finally realized her ticket to reaching her life goals with vigor while maintaining functional and cognitive health required a "healthy lifestyle". She committed to rigorous disease prevention studies and quality of life integration which turned her health and lifestyle **180º**.

Maria understands the strain of a busy and stressful life. Maria creates **personalized** experiences and programs for **single clients, families, groups, and organizations**. Her **E.N.E.R.G.Y. System** along with her guidance, accountability, motivation, and tools transforms lives from the inside out. She has helped clients overcome struggles with weight, fatigue, burnout, belly fat, brain fog, insulin resistance, blood sugar and hormone imbalances. Step-by-step, she educates her clients in smart nutritional choices, management of stress and sleep, fitness and strength, and mindfulness. What sets Maria apart is that she offers a complete wellness solution, a 20+ year career in international business and finance, and a unique ability to identify and help remove 'debris' from their paths.

Maria earned her Executive MBA from Emory University. She completed Health Coaching training at Precision Nutrition and the Institute of Nutritional Endocrinology. There, she completed the Insulin Resistance Practitioner Training and is training in Nutritional Endocrinology. She received training in Personal Training at National Academy of Sports Medicine.

Maria is **virtual**--coaching and training by video conference and phone. In-person, she **comes to you** or you come to her in Atlanta, GA. **No Excuse! At Work. At Home. Be Fab - Be You!**

Reinvent Yourself

by Maria Horstmann

> *"Do not exchange what you want the most*
> *for what you want in the moment."*

In 1996, at age 21, I left Brazil, my family, my college education, a dream job, and a 3-year relationship for an internship in Atlanta, GA. My intentions were to learn and return home to apply the new skills. Fast forward to 2018, I own a house in Atlanta, earned a B.A. in finance, and graduated with honors at Emory's Executive MBA program. Between age 21 and 40, I travelled the world and embarked on adventures of a lifetime. I started a business after I changed my health lifestyle, and career 180º

Today, I have had the honor to educate and transform the lives of people worldwide. I help them set and achieve their health goals to discover, become, and live their best self. Despite all, there was a time I was sick inside, felt like a loser, lost, and lonely.

I lived most of life with chronic constipation, gastrointestinal issues, highly addicted to sugar and prediabetes. Times of pain, embarrassment, and brutally emotional. I experienced unparalleled cravings, binging, and purging. High sugary foods, caffeine and energy drinks supplied 'energy' to perform at work and as compensation for inadequate sleep. I played volleyball, ate junk food, and drank alcohol to manage stress, anger, and mood swings. That lifestyle was slowly destroying my body and mind. I was well educated, yet clueless.

At age 36, my mother asked whether I wanted to age childless - who would help me? I spent weeks assessing family history, health risk, personal habits, emotions, needs, and desires. Finally, I understood that implementing a healthy lifestyle was my new beginning. Plus, I wanted to age content with cognitive and functional health and minimize risks of dementia, cancer, and reappearence of depression.

I researched, read books, and joined health summits. I became obsessed about hormones function, energy production, and brain health. Overcoming my sugar addiction was one of the hardest things I ever did. The struggle was real. I 'argued' with my brain daily. I debated why/what/when, buy or not, eat or not the candy, chocolate, ice cream, pastry. No matter the strategy I planned, I always lost the battle. After hundreds of hours of education and nutritional improvements, I began to gain control and win the battles. My personal transformation led me to believe I could help others and I went on to get formal training.

I am committed to this journey. I want people to win their battle with more ease. I am passionate about teaching and I talk my walk. I learned how to unstuck, to push past my fears, to press reset, to have tough conversations, and redesign my life. Big part of transforming our bodies starts with transforming our thought process.

A great example is my former client Melissa. She came to me for weight loss. This successful pediatric orthopedic surgeon in her late 30's, lost self-esteem, motivation, and discipline. We spent most of our time re-programming her mindset, uncovering limiting beliefs, establishing routines and boundaries, and managing to boost energy and confidence to implement other essential health protocols. In three months, she lost 10% body weight and redefined herself. I teared up when she said *'Thank you. **You changed my life forever.'***

Today, I am free of my symptoms, energetic, confident, clear-headed physically, emotionally, and mentally strong. My experiences, failures, and triumphs enrich my relationships, life, and practice. Each person I educate, inspire, and transform gives me energy, fulfillment, contentment, and a sense of freedom. These feelings I want everyone in the world to experience daily as well.

* * *

Maria Horstmann
BeFabBeYou.com
770-835-5490
mhorstmann@BeFabBeYou.com

Cynthia Higgins, MD

Motivational Speaker
Psychiatrist
Integrated Energy Therapist

Cynthia Higgins, MD

BIOGRAPHY

What makes Cynthia so different is her willingness to receive information from non-traditional sources and apply that wisdom in a manner that cuts to the heart of what her patients need for healing.

Seldom do we hear of *'intuition' in a medical setting.* Yet, Cynthia discovered during her years as a medical researcher, and as a provider of traditional and alternative approaches, is that our unconscious mind plays a greater role in our lives than we ever thought possible. She often states that she dwells in the world of the "psycho-spiritual". She recognizes how intimately our physical and emotional well-being is related to our belief systems, spiritual and otherwise. When a thought or emotion creates changes in the expression of DNA, it is referred to as an *'epigenetic influence'.*

Cynthia aspires to increase global awareness of how applying this knowledge can improve thousands of lives affected by chronic conditions.

Cynthia is the 5th child of a business owner and educator; her mother remains one of her greatest influences. *"She worked a full time job during the day and scrubbed floors and toilets at night while I slept to put herself through graduate school to make a better life for her family".* Inspired by her mother's determination, Cynthia earned a Bachelor of Arts in Molecular Biology from Princeton University. While studying for a Master's degree in Biochemistry at the University of Miami, she was accepted into the University of South Florida College of Medicine. She completed her Medical Internship at Duke University before returning to the University of South Florida to complete training in General Psychiatry and Fellowship in Child and Adolescent Psychiatry.

Cynthia's work experience includes medical research, private and public health psychiatry. Recently, she was designed Top Energy Psychiatrist 2019 by the International Association of Top Professionals for her remarkable work in integrating mental health, spiritual and quantum physics principals in the care of her patients.

The Miracle Within

by Cynthia Higgins

"Our greatest potential lies not in our accomplishments, but in the magnificence of our authentic selves. Embracing this, we become the creative alchemists of our own existence, capable of transforming the mundane, into the extraordinary".

Our lives tell a story, times of struggle and of triumph. Each story is replete with symbolism that seeks to align and empower us if we are patient, courageous and trusting enough to listen. My goal is to help others hasten to that voice of truth and shed light on a beauty that is often overlooked. I long ago recognized that one of the greatest gifts I could offer to another is a shift in perspective. The impact of this shift can be the difference between thriving and despair.

When quantum physicists followed their study of matter to the smallest particle, a surprising discovery was made. What became as intriguing as the particle itself was the force controlling it: perception. Among its many definitions, perception is defined as "a way of regarding, understanding or interpreting something". It is also defined as the neurophysiological process, including memory, by which an organism becomes aware of and interprets stimuli.

If a particle in a lab study can respond to the expectations of its observers, what does this say about us, beings composed of trillions of cells and particles? What layer of complexity is added when we embrace an array of beliefs, Spiritual and otherwise? How would our lives change if our genetics plays only a portion of the role we once thought?

The medical research that has measured the effect of our thoughts, most notably, those combined with emotion, suggests that we have at our disposal a personal power that serves as an unfailing navigation towards our hearts' desires. It can also serve to guide us away from actions based on imagined fear.

An ever increasing body of evidence exists to support the fact that our beliefs(perceptions) initiate a cascade of electrophysiological, hormonal and biochemical events that not only affect our emotions, but can affect behavior, immune function, pain sensitivity and cellular repair.

Knowing this, I like to create a collaborative alliance with others Where we start with the symptoms and work our way back to the limiting belief that may act as fuel poured onto the fire of a genetic predisposition already present for depression, anxiety or physical illness. Using traditional as well as a variety of alternative medicine approaches, we then act to interpret the meaning behind patterns of negative life experiences. Once the relevance of these events or symptoms within the context of an individual's belief system is understood, it allows for the adoption of empowering actions that promote growth and change.

My approach to healing therefore represents an uncommon paradigm that has required carving inroads on three simultaneous fronts. First, when I am told *"No one has ever listened or taken time to talk to me the way you have."* it speaks as much about us as providers as it does about patients, and sadly, we have accepted this as the way things are. Our perspectives, on both sides of the medical field regarding what is possible is often the greatest obstacle to the vigor with which we approach the management of mental health issues.

Secondly, uncovering limiting beliefs can be challenging. From homemakers to physicians, our inspiration and our courage to affect changes in our lives can be undermined by what we hold as a society to be acceptable or good. This drive to belong and conform is an instinct born of the fact that at one time, our individual survival depended upon acceptance by the greater whole.

Even today we fear being rejected greater than we fear the consequences of not listening to our own intuition because we have never been taught to value the one priceless thing we can all own. Often this need for acceptance creates such desperation and fear that we are willing to compromise *everything that makes us unique.* We can allow an opportunity to pass us by, fearing that the change it would make in our world would render us unaccepted or unrecognizable to ourselves; we stay in our toxic interactions and invalidating experiences despite knowing the price we pay in the currency of our happiness.

What I do seeks to give a voice to those that traditionally don't feel heard. It provides choices for those who historically have felt they have none: I have known generations in which the presence of mental health problems cannot be mentioned, while the same families succumb to preventable physical diseases, never once considering that the two might actually be related.

Much like nearly everything associated with mental functioning, we have been taught to fear what may well be one of our greatest strengths. I believe that those instances of distress caused by an intolerable work environment, abusive romantic relationships or other circumstances where we are forced to give up a vital part of ourselves don't constitute "weakness" as it is commonly believed. As painful as these events can be, they also represent potential awakenings for our consciousness. The magnitude of this awakening is limited only by our attachment to the very thing that we may have outgrown.

When we miss or ignore the earlier communications, the physical and emotional challenges we face can sometimes be the final common pathway in a mind-body-spirit interaction which signals that it is time for a radical change in our beliefs and practices. The more technological we have become, the more popular it is to value logic over intuition, and as a society, it has hurt us tremendously. Who exactly, is this thief in the night who has stolen away our happiness? We are absolutely masterful at getting stuck in our own heads. We create an analysis thought-loop that eliminates

Cynthia Higgins

all of our options and leaves us in a state of panic and despair. More than anything, intuition is a love or heart-centered Knowing, involving our entire physiology and the full spectrum of our consciousness.

If we cannot honor our own intuition and find peace within ourselves, how can we possibly expect to experience harmony with others? We know that the electrical field generated by our heart is at least 10 times larger than that generated by our brain. Whereas our brain can alert us to a danger or opportunity the moment it happens, our intuition can notify us days or even weeks before this occurs.

By incorporating intuition into their decision making, students in my classes report improvements in their depression or anxiety independent of their medication status. Others state that they become "unstuck" and better attuned to their life goals. I feel fortunate to help bridge the illustration of separation between science, our diverse spiritualities, our intuition and our experiences.

As a speaker and educator, my purpose is to increase awareness of our impressive potential; to switch the lens of our focus from our limitations to the growth that is possible when we honor ourselves in our true authenticity. We are our own greatest resource and appreciating ourselves and each other is paramount if we are to thrive as individual and as a nation.

* * *

Cynthia Higgins, MD
928-301-7664
www.Serenityservicesfl.com
chiggins1806@gmail.com

Nicole Caley

Chief Executive Optimist

Living Virtuously, LLC

Business Woman, Motivational Speaker
Mentor, Advocate for Girls and Women

Nicole Caley

BIOGRAPHY

Nicole Caley could have easily become just another statistic in the teenage mom, absentee father narrative - where a quality education, mental and emotional stability, self-confidence, and a safe home were things she could have only dreamed of having. Fortunately for Nicole, it was those exact statistics that drove her to become "anything but her family".

As a dynamic, results-driven leader, Nicole has demonstrated success as the Director of several operational accounting teams, and while she is extremely committed to her role, the development of others, and being of service to them, Nicole's true passion is dedicated to serving the Chicagoland area through True Mentors, Women's Leadership efforts, as well as private speaking engagements. She specifically focuses on the inner city of Chicago and the young girls there. Her hunger to serve girls and women has prompted her to establish Living Virtuously LLC, focusing her efforts in motivational speaking and helping young girls triumph after being sexually abused.

Throughout her illustrious career Nicole has received awards, accolades and has been recognized worldwide for her outstanding leadership and commitment to her profession and service to others.

For 2019 she is being considered for a feature in Top Industry Professional Magazine and for the Top Female Executive Award by the International Association of Top Professionals(IAOTP). For 2018 she was selected as Top Professional of the Year in Finance and Management by IAOTP. In 2017 Nicole was selected as Outstanding Professional of the Year by the National Association of Professional women, and in 2016 she was awarded AP Director of the Year for Organizations >$1b by the Institute of Finance and Management. She is the President of the Board of the Illinois Chapter of the Institute of Finance and Management, member of the National Speakers Association, and member of the Board of Directors for True Mentors, where she is an active servant/mentor for girls and women nationally.

You Always Have a Choice!

Who you are is what you chose to be!

by Nicole Caley

"I do not regret any decision I have made, nor feel shame about things that have happened to me, for they have all made me what I am today."

Every day I remind people that the greatest part of life is that we have a choice. You can choose to be happy or angry, be a victim or a survivor, be selfless or selfish, tell the truth or lie - but at the end of the day, you always have a choice, and no one can take that away from you without your permission.

Like many others, I have experienced great pain and sadness in my life. For some, calamity comes in their adult years, for me it started when I was just a child. I was born to a teenage mom, an absentee father, and was raised by my grandmother, who struggled as a single mom not only to raise her children, but her grandchild as well. There were many days we had no heat or hot water, or utilities were turned off for non-payment. I would be sent to give the utility company a check that we knew wouldn't clear the bank just to have service restored. At the time, I thought this was "normal".

At the age of five, I began to be molested by my neighbor, a married man with two children of his own who were just slightly older than me. This continued for five years, and I remember the countless times I would beg my grandma not to send me there, however, she had to work to pay the bills, and there were not many options for a babysitter. It didn't help that he worked for the city I grew up in, so even if something was said, nothing would be done about it. Eventually, I began to feel like I was doing my part in taking care of the household, until one day, I could not take it anymore, and threatened to tell the school if she sent me back.

Fast forward a few years, I started to spend more time with my mother, who spent the majority of her time on the West and South sides of Chicago - these neighborhoods hold the highest crime and murder rates in the city. There I learned how to turn cocaine into crack, shoot a gun, and drive a getaway car for gang activity gone wrong. But that wasn't the worst of it, at the age of 16, I witnessed two people I knew very well get shot; one twice in the head, and the other seven times throughout his body. I sat on the ground, covered in their blood, holding one of them waiting **sixteen minutes** for the paramedics to arrive. Only one of them survived.

It was then that I decided I was going to use my life experiences to help others. I had a choice - be a victim of my circumstances, yes some I chose, or use those circumstances to promote **choice** and advocate for others.

What shocks people the most is that through all I've just shared, I always remained top of my class academically, retained perfect attendance in school, and was an activist for breaking down racial barriers in my predominately upper-class, white community. It was almost as though I lived a double life.

Accepting Personal Responsibility

At a young age I learned that each of us has a personal responsibility for our life, and my first choice was to be everything my family was not. I had poor role models for a functional adult relationship, little priority of education, and lived in a completely dishonest and secretive environment. I grew up oblivious to what love should be - my mom was more like a sister (when she felt like it), my father was out of the picture, and my grandma allowed me to be molested.

All I ever wanted was to be different - and I am. I chose to accept the things that happened in my life, but did not allow them to define who I am. As a teenager, I was already making plans as to how I was going to assist other young girls and women conquer the embarrassment, depression, fear, and anxiety of being molested or raped. All too often women do not deal with the emotional effects because it is too difficult - I help them to realize that holding it in is more often even more damaging. Together, I support them in not allowing the tragedy to define them. It's a choice.

Every Choice Has a Consequence.

Clearly, I have not always made the best choices - but I have learned from them. I am grateful for my time spent in the inner city of Chicago as a teenager because it allowed me to break racial barriers that all too often exist. It is the reason I can support the young girls at the Ark of Saint Sabina in Chicago's Englewood community - because although I don't look like I fit in, I can relate.

Whether your choices end with your initial desired outcome, or something completely different - don't be ashamed of them. Determine what you can learn from them and apply it to future decisions, or use it as a launch pad to help others.

In my day job, people complain every day - it's human nature. My response is always the same, "you have a choice". In most cases, I am met with the typical blanket "I have bills to pay" response, but I stand firm. You have a choice. Now, whether or not you like the consequence is not for me to decide. If you do not like something, change it - if you cannot change it, stop complaining about it or remove yourself from the situation, But never should your response be that you don't have a choice, because you always do. It's up to you to act on it.

Your Current Situation Does Not Dictate Your Future.

Statistically I should have been a teenage mom, on welfare, with a high school level education, if I were lucky enough to be alive. Fortunately for me, none of that turned true. I am 37, on my way to marrying an incredible man, we have no children, I hold three degrees, and my success has been nothing short of a dream come true. I decided a long time ago that my situation was not going to define me nor stifle my ability to impact the world.

I could have decided to be the victim of childhood molestation, where my self-confidence and self-worth had been destroyed. I'd be lying if I said there aren't days I question my self-worth because of the lack of genuine love I received as a child, but I make a conscious choice to overcome those days.

I could have decided to become involved with the gangs, drugs, and violence that was so prevalent in my teenage years, but I knew I had more to offer the world. I could have decided not to go to college at the age of 28, because it would be too difficult to work full time and go to school, but I felt a degree was the only way I'd be important enough to change the world. I was wrong!

The point is - you have a choice. Are you going to allow your current circumstances to dictate your future or are you going to fight like hell to be different, defy the odds, and be a conqueror? I'm not saying it will always be easy - nothing worth having is - but I can promise you, you won't regret the fight! You've probably heard the old adage, "that's the way the cookie crumbles", but I challenge that your cookie doesn't have to crumble - that's **your choice to make!**

* * *

Nicole Caley
(833) 4-VIRTUE
nicole@livingvirtuously.net
www.livingvirtuously.net

COURAGE

It is easy to be courageous when life is treating you well. But when you are met with experiences that test your faith, when plans go astray and hurts sadden~hope wanes. It is a time of no guarantees, a time of uncertainty, and perhaps even chaos.

Life sometimes appears hopelessly confused; but there are no wounds that cannot be healed, no matter how deep, or permanent they seem. You persevere not only for yourself but for those who look to you for guidance and inspiration.

Every principle you have ever studied and every experience you have ever had is called upon to stretch your courage to heights you were unaware were within your reach. It is true that if you keep fear from moving in, you find resources at your command that you never dreamt possible.

You become a master at generating self-inspiration. When you feel inspired everything changes. There are no longer conflicts - all is as it should be. You become aligned with the knowledge that the answers you seek are on the way. Your inner being - the core of your strength - whispers: "Hold on. You'll make it."

Courage doesn't dwell on the impossibility of anything. If there were no magic in the power of believing, you would soon stop believing. But you don't. You go on in the face of overwhelming odds that transform circumstances beyond physical explanation. Even if your world crumbles, you have the power to put it back together and with renewed faith move in an increasingly positive direction to enrich your life.

Leah M. Williams

Supply Chain Planning Specialist
Northrop Grumman Corporation

Leah M. Williams

BIOGRAPHY

Leah Williams is an outstanding leader, a talented professional, and a phenomenal young woman.

When Leah graduated from Delaware State University in 2015, She made history, as the first person to ever be awarded both the **Presidential Academic Award for her cumulative 4.0 GPA,** and the **Presidential Leadership Award for her campus leadership.** Leah completed her MBA the following year and currently works as a Supply Chain Analyst for Northrop Grumman.

Leah has received a number of honors, and has been recognized worldwide for her outstanding leadership, performance, and service to the community. For 2017, Leah was selected as one of the top 30 under 30 Rising Supply Chain Stars in the Country by Thomas/ISM. In 2018, Leah was recognized as the top Supply Chain Analyst of the Year by IAOTP. Leah has been featured on Aspire TV Network, the HBCU Nation Radio Show, Spend Matters, and other media networks.

After being diagnosed with Crohn's disease at the age of 22, Leah serves as an advocate and strives to be an inspiration to others who are battling illness. Leah is also an advocate for Historically Black Colleges & Universities. **Leah was selected by the White House in 2015, to serve as an HBCU All Star supporting President Obama's initiative to promote the excellence, innovation, and sustainability of HBCUs. Leah introduced Vice President Biden at the HBCU Week Conference.** In addition, Leah currently serves as the Vice President of DSU's National Alumni Association and in 2016, DSU selected Leah as one of their Top Under/Over 40 Alumni.

Leah uses her abilities to inspire and impact others, as an excellent speaker, scholar, advocate, and more! A lifelong learner, Leah has continued to further her education by obtaining both the PMP & CSCP Certifications. A gifted musician, Leah plays nine instruments and arranges music. Leah plans to keep making her mark on the world and in her community any way she can.

Making Our Mark on the World

A Call to Action

by Leah Williams

"Make a Mark on the World One Heart at a time."

In 2015, at the age of 22, I was diagnosed with Crohn's disease, an autoimmune disease which affects the entire digestive track. I had recently graduated from undergrad, and had just began my Master's program. Young, happy, and healthy; with my whole life in front of me, I was excited to take on the world. Suddenly, one day a stomach pain turned into a life-changing diagnosis.

Growing up, I never imagined I would face health issues. I always admired the strength of those who battled diseases, but never imagined being in similar shoes. After the diagnosis, I knew my life would never be the same. At that moment I had two options, I could use the disease as a crutch, or I could use the disease as motivation.

"Making Our Mark on the World" Is the official slogan of my 2x Alma Mater Delaware State University. This Slogan transcended my college years, as I adopted it as my mantra for life. To me, it represents a call to action; a call that never ends, as there are always new ways to keep making my mark on the world.

A "mark" can come in all shapes and sizes. A mark can be small or large, short or long. A mark can be temporary, or last forever. Each of us has our own way of making our mark(s) on the world. Life is our journey to finding ourselves, our purpose, and to leave as many marks as possible. A mark can also be positive or negative, but the type of mark we leave is truly our decision. The actions we take, the attitudes we display, and the resources we share, all affect the marks we leave.

Living with a disease is constantly facing your biggest challenge every day. Diseases are unpredictable, and each morning you are unsure of whether you will be facing a peak or valley on its physical and emotional roller coaster. Through all of the ups and downs, I find comfort in having the constant reminder to make my mark on the world. Each and every one of us faces our own unique challenges; Each and every one of us has the ability to make our marks on the world.

Over the years, many people have made a positive mark in my life. These marks have encouraged me to become who I am today. The marks came in a variety of forms and were left by a diverse group of people. Whether the marks were in the form of a story or advice, or even in the form of an inspirational dance, a kind word, or smile. Whether the marks were left by a teacher or friend, a family member or stranger. I will forever be thankful to those who took the time to positively impact my life.

By touching the hearts of those in our community, at work, and especially in the next generation, I know we can all positively make our marks on the world. Every time we interact with someone, is an opportunity to make a positive mark. Whether it is for a split second, an hour, or all day; there are plenty of opportunities to leave a mark. The more cognizant we are of the marks we make, the more effort we can place into making sure the marks we leave are positive. We can utilize our talents, our strengths, and our experiences to make our marks. You never know when the mark you leave is going to inspire someone for the better. My challenge to us all: *let's all make our marks on the world, one heart at a time.*

* * *

Leah Williams
leah.m.williams@outlook.com

Geri Gibbons

Life Strategy Coach
G Gibbons Coaching, LLC

Geri Gibbons

BIOGRAPHY

Life strategy coach Geri Gibbons works with smart, successful women whose quality of life and relationships are dogged by issues of weight, perfectionism and lack of confidence.

Think of her as your personal change agent.

"Managing mindset helps women crack the code of so many issues that get in the way of what we want. Feelings of not being enough, of not living the life you want, of feeling 'stuck,' - those are the issues my clients want to overcome. They want to live with purpose, meaning, and joy."

Geri lived the struggle herself. Until, that is, she discovered the connection between the physical and mental. She personally used the cognitive coaching tools she shares with her clients to lose more than 35 lbs, leave behind past trauma, and create a successful business.

"These tools helped me understand why I was overeating, develop a healthy body image, and recapture my joy and energy," said Geri.

Geri received a Bachelor of Science from the London School of Economics & Political Science, graduating with honors in economics and international relations. After 25 years working in corporate marketing for US and UK corporations, Geri shifted professional gears to life coaching in 2016. She holds professional certifications in life coaching and weight loss coaching from prestigious 'The Life Coach School'.

What convinced her to make that change? After experiencing the difference life coaching made in her own life, Geri left her corporate job to do more coaching and mentoring. She wanted to give back. "I work with women and meet them right where they are," said Geri. "We all need to start somewhere, and one of my favorite things is to help women get 'unstuck'."

Today Geri is fueled by a passion to share this work with women who think they are not "enough" in some way.

What are you hiding behind?

Leave self-doubt behind to create lasting change

by Geri Gibbons

"Change happens when you let go of the past and fall in love with your future"

I was a smart, successful woman with an impressive resume. It was not a facade ... it's just that I was also hiding behind...

- **Work.** I was the get-it-done go-to-woman at work, caught up in receiving awards and accolades.

- **Family.** It took a village to keep my home life afloat, while I piled on the hours at work. This go-to, get-it-done gal was hiding despair, confusion, and maybe a little depression on the inside.

- **Weight.** I could not lose weight and keep it off. I was secretly afraid something was deeply flawed in me.

Sound Familiar? I became a life coach because, after years of weight weight loss programs (you name it, I tried it) and therapy, I discovered the answer to "what's wrong with me." It was so pivotal that I am compelled to share what I've learned with other women like me. Want to know what it was? ***Nothing***

There was nothing "wrong with me." I discovered that I had the power to choose. I discovered that what I thought about directly affected my feelings, and it was life-changing for me. It fueled a passion in me to share this knowledge with my corporate sisters, my fellow working mamas, and solo parents.

I did all the right things, but life happened anyway.

As a young woman, I did all the things I thought I would guarantee a smooth, carefree life. I went to a great university and landed an amazing job at "the" global investment firm of the day.   My career was going well. And then I took a job at another firm where, for nine months, I was the target of daily verbal and sexual abuse.   I finally gathered up the

250

courage to walk out the door of that job and that industry. The only things that I took with me were a debilitating case of PTSD and about 25 extra pounds of fat.

Time, distance, and a new career in publishing helped restore peace and sanity to my life. I worked for strong, smart, decisive female executives, including the formidable, phenomenal CEO Dame Gail Rebuck. I saw women who defined the term "stand in their own power." I wanted what they had, but I had no idea how to get it. Instead I worked extra hard so no one would notice the chasm of unworthiness I felt.

Eventually, I went to work for PwC. Within three years I become the youngest marketing director in the firm. I moved back to the U.S. -First to Miami, then Boston and finally back to my hometown, Madison, WI. Everywhere I moved, I took myself with me. Now at Deloitte, I worked extra hard. I earned accolades, awards, and bonuses. But I struggled with thoughts like "What's wrong with me?" and "Isn't there something else?"

Although my professional career was soaring, I continued to struggle with an ongoing battle with my weight. I lost weight, regained it, added to it, and lost it again - over and over. So despite great career success and overcoming my own #metoo story, I was overweight and unfulfilled.

I found my answers in life coaching.

All those "I'm not good enough" beliefs shattered. With the help of cognitive-based life coaching techniques, I learned what I now teach clients: how to deal with challenging jobs, colleagues, and workplaces, relationships and THE STUFF OF life so they can feel good again.

My life today is not perfect, but I'm charting my own course and it's a good life. Hiding no more. Standing in my own power.

* * *

Geri Gibbons
608-501-2719
coach@gerigibbons.com
www.gerigibbons.com

Anita R. Minor-Clifford

Lender/Investor
Unlimited Commercial Financing Group, LLC

Anita R. Minor-Clifford

BIOGRAPHY

Anita Robyn Minor-Clifford is the owner of Unlimited Commercial Financing Group, LLC and 3KLA Realty Investors. She works as a Commercial Finance Consultant and a Real Estate Investor.

Anita received her certification as a Christian Financial Consultant in 2002, which is her true passion to teach and help people to comprehend and understand how to manage their personal finances by facing their Goliath (giant) face on.

She also loves to share on the importance of saving, giving and striving to be dept free, which should be a goal for everyone. A saying that Anita has is "If you don't save, you won't have anything." Anita has spoken on personal finances for Women's Conferences, Prayer Breakfast, and for Workshops. Sharing with all ages from children as young as 10 and older.

From 2007-2008 Anita established the Financial Freedom Group (FFG) that offered a complete debt elimination program for individuals and families. Already having a desire to help people with their finances and to get out of debt, the creation of FFG was exciting to her.

Anita is currently Financial Secretary at her local church where she has assisted the treasurer with financial duties for over 15 years.

Anita also worked in the IT field as an Application Developer for the federal government as a government employee and contractor for over 25 years.

In addition to speaking and sharing on finances, she enjoys liturgical dancing as the President of one of her church's dance ministries, collecting banks of all sorts, and Thomas Kinkade(The Painter of Light) paintings as a hobby.

Anita currently resides in Clinton, MD with her husband Lavant and their three children Krystal, Kayla and Kaaman and their dog Speedy. She has been a resident of Prince George's County since 1984.

The Fear is Real

But Don't Let That Stop You
by Anita R. Minor-Clifford

"In all labor there is profit, but mere talk leads to poverty"
Proverbs 14:23

As an Entrepreneur, I tried many business opportunities in my lifetime. Real Estate Investment thus far has been the most adventurous, challenging and educational. At first, I had no desire to buy, fix and flip homes or buy in the Baltimore, MD area. I wanted to invest my money into other Real Estate Investor's projects and make a profit; as referred to in real estate training, "Rinse and Repeat". So how did I get here? My first investment property in West Baltimore, MD and a MAJOR HEAVY-DUTY rehab project! Really???

The Fear is Real became my mantra. I was on the emotional roller coaster ride of my life. Literally, happy one day, crying and full of anxiety the next; excited the next, back to crying full of fear the next. My mind going a mile as I tried vainly to sleep. No rest or peace. Praying all the time. What should I do with this property? Wholesale it? Keep it? Fix and flip it? Rent it? What should I do? At times I thought, "I don't like this ride anymore - and I want to get off." However, the train had left the station so there was no was no turning back. So, sit back, buckle up and enjoy the ride!

In business there are always risks and everyone has a different risk tolerance level. Some people have low risk tolerance, some moderate, and others have a high risk tolerance. Which one are you? We are familiar with the saying **"No risk No reward"**. Very true. I just never realized I was so audacious. So, that places me in the HIGH risk category. Just call me: **Scurry, from "Who moved My Cheese?"** I have my tennis shoes tied around my neck always ready to go! My goal though is to become more like **Sniff, definately not Hem or Haw.**

Working in Real Estate Investment you have all kinds of challenges: funding, staying on budget, hiring good contractors, trusting people, time management, deadlines and overall just making wise decisions. You can have these challenges in any type of endeavor or in life. Fear can be felt in many different situations, but don't let that stop you. If you do, you miss out on the rewards.

Throughout life we all experience a roller coaster ride of ups and downs, upside down and swirled all around. But I firmly believe every challenge, hurdle, road block and set back is a lesson learned. These lessons make us a little better, more confident, wiser, smarter and stronger. That's why it's so important to give it your best shot and not let FEAR - (Fear of Evidence that Appears Real) stop you. My shot is HEAVY-DUTY rehab project in Baltimore, MD. I have no doubt my project will be a tremendous success and I will reap the rewards.

The fear of failure is gone. My confidence has grown though roadblocks remain. I have learned a lot and for that I am grateful. I'm a lot smarter and wiser now. I have peace and rest well. Yes, there may be more set - backs to overcome. But this I know— It can and will be done, it's worth the risk!

God Bless!!!

* * *

Anita R. Minor-Clifford
301-922-3695
ucfgllc@gmail.com

Celeste
Johnson-Matheson

CEO - KEEP ME NEAR THE CROSS
Award Winning Inspirational Author

Celeste Johnson-Matheson

BIOGRAPHY

Celeste is an Award-winning author, inspirational speaker, and Executive Liaison Officer for the US Government.

Celeste Johnson-Matheson, CEO, Keep Me Near the Cross (K.M.N.T.C.), LLC, has been recognized with the Excellence Award as a Distinguished Professional in her field by the Women of Distinction Magazine 2016/2017.

"I believe we all have a unique God-given talent to share with the rest of the world." Celeste's leap of faith shines through with her first book: **Keep Me Near the Cross: Judgement or Journey?** by JAHS Publishing Group. The true-to-life novel focuses on every-day struggles Christians face. The book was so successful Celeste built an entire business around its philosophy.

"I want people to read my book and know that their life challenges are a platform for opportunities. The challenges are not the issue; it's how you respond to those challenges. Your mindset determines the outcome. Use your life adversities to help others, for opportunities, and personal growth."

Keep Me Near the Cross: Judgement or Journey? was honored with the "Finalist Award" religion category as Best Book Int'l 2018 and 2017 by the American Book Fest. Celeste is completing her second novel titled **Hold Me Jesus: Love Conquers All** released later this year.

Celeste's future plans include starting a non-profit organization to provide books to kids in under-served communities. ***"When GOD blesses you; you have an obligation to share those blessings with others."***

* * *

Celeste Johnson-Matheson
(703)944-9554
celestejohnson.author@gmail.com
www.keepmenearthecross.com

Demetria Davenport

Founder & Owner
Luxurious Essentials Travel Day Spa

Demetria Davenport

BIOGRAPHY

Demetria Davenport is the founder of Luxurious Essentials Travel Day Spa. Her inspiration took root 16 years ago while attending Michigan College of Beauty where she earned a manicure license. Prior, she was employed by a pharmaceutical company for 11 years; but she yearned to become an entrepreneur in charge of her own destiny.

Demetria launched Luxurious Essentials in May 2007. She studied massage therapy at Stasios Institute of Therapeutic Massage and earned certification in 2008. Demetria is passionate about massage therapy treatments for chronic and acute conditions, with emphasis on neck, shoulder and back dysfunction due to auto and sports injuries. She is certified in pain management specializing in shoulder rehabilitation, vestibular assessment and treatment, joint replacement, and orthopedic massage techniques for cervical pain.

Demetria listens and involves her clients so that they work together in coming up with the best treatment to ensure their hope and goals are met. As a Health Practitioner, Demetria focuses on general wellness, educating clients on the benefits of exercise, nutrition, and positive thinking to create a well-balanced lifestyle. She also incorporates remedial exercises into a home care plan that can be easily incorporated into a daily routine.

Demetria has been featured in numerous publications including the cover story of Women of Distinction Magazine. She is an accredited member of the Better Business Bureau 2016 - 2018. Demetria was honored with five awards for Best Massage Therapy Company in Southfield, MI 2014 - 2018. She's also an Alumni of Goldman Sachs 10,000 small businesses.

Demetria is an inspiring example of someone who believed in her dreams and won. She 'gives back' by mentoring young women who aspire to succeed in the beauty business. In her free time she is an avid reader, travels, and spends quality time with family.

My Version of Success
Creating My Own Path

by Demetria Davenport

> *"Self-belief and hard work will always earn you success."*
> *-Virat Kohli*

The values and work ethics my parents instilled in me - little did I realize then - prepared me for the entrepreneurial journey. For me stepping out on faith was scary but exciting at the same time. I was fine with the fact that my financial security would be no more. I knew once I made the transition to create my own path there would be no turning back. As an entrepreneur, I was master of my own destiny.

At a young age, my parents always encouraged me and my siblings that in this country we could be anything we wanted to be - but most importantly, to be the best at whatever we did. My mother was big on education, however, if college wasn't our chosen path, she stressed the importance of self-reliance, whether with a job, joining the service, or starting our own business.

Years later, when I became an entrepreneur it was hard to find a mentor. So I read every book I could find about business, entrepreneurship and how to establish a day spa. I found salons were more sociable and busy, while the spa setting offered a more tranquil and relaxing atmosphere.

After extensive research, a brick-and-mortar spa was not in the budget; so I came up with the concept of a Traveling Day Spa. I have always been an innovator - thinking outside of the box - and this idea was new with an untapped market. As time passed, I opened my first location in Southfield, MI. to help others escape the hustle and bustle and feel more relaxed and rejuvenated to handle the challenges of everyday life.

People often ask how I survived this long with all the ups-and-downs of an entrepreneurial beauty business. My reply is that my mother always said, *"believe in yourself and never be a quitter".*

I keep that foremost in my mind always, especially during the past four years with a 9-5 job to keep my business going "against all odds."

What it takes to be an entrepreneur and build a great business can be very challenging, and a test of faith. For five months. I had to temporarily close the doors due to some compliance issues around the building I leased. To stay up and running and relevant I worked at another establishment for a while. This was a difficult time for me - servicing clients, meeting legal requirements, and looking for a new location. But, I stayed focused and kept the faith that my business would survive. **And it did!**

The most essential strength of any successful entrepreneur is passion and purpose. I am big on both. Otherwise, I would have reached a breaking point - given up and lost my dream forever. But the fire and determination I naturally possess kept me going. I thought about how far I had come and *nothing* real or imagined could sway me off course. Giving up was not an option. What mattered was to see my vision through. I am truly invigorated by the positive events that keep happening every day.

I want to encourage every entrepreneur who has a dream and the innovative spirit to launch one ... *never give up!* If the path is not obvious, create your own path and take action toward your aspirational journey and goal. And, one day, surely your vision will become reality!

* * *

Demetria Davenport
(313)655-3860
www.letravelspa.com
Demetria@letravelspa.com

Carolyn Stowers Harris

President

Young Entrepreneurs of the Future, Inc. (YEF)

Carolyn Stowers Harris

BIOGRAPHY

Carolyn Stowers Harris fulfilled her childhood desire to establish an organization that provides disadvantaged urban teenagers with the necessary life skills to succeed in our competitive society.

Carolyn left her position at IRS, after experiencing chronic health issues, and personally funded Young Entrepreneurs of the Future, Inc. (YEF) a 501 (c)(3) non - profit mentoring, coaching, advocacy and entrepreneurship training organization in 1991, with help from her son, four of his friends, support from parents and business leaders.

"I was greatly saddened to learn that urban teenagers have the highest rates of unemployment and need extra support and education to help get them on a career pathway. Young Entrepreneurs of the Future, Inc. (YEF), started with youth for youth to help provide that extra support teenagers need."

Carolyn involved the teenagers in ownership of the program through hands - on - job experiences, while having a voice in the decision-making process. "Young Entrepreneurs of the Future's summer work program helps teenagers become assets to their families and communities by working, earning wages, paying taxes, and not becoming part of gang violence and crime in their neighborhoods."

Carolyn received her Non-profit Administrator Certification from the University of Pennsylvania; and Master Certification in Human Resource Management from Michigan State University; The National Association for Teaching Entrepreneurship at the Wharton Business School.

In 2016 Carolyn created and hosted the extremely popular Young Entrepreneurs Radio Show on BBM Global Network and Tunein Radio. She recruited guests from local colleges and entrepreneurs from around the nation to share successful experiences as YEF alumni, and how they became role models.

Helping Our Youth

Removing Barriers for Teenagers

by Carolyn Stowers Harris

"Commit to the Lord whatever you do, and your plans will
succeed. He works out everything for his own ends."
Proverbs 16:3

I pray each day. I try to set aside a few minutes, usually at the
end of the day, to think over the events of the day and their
significance. The question I put to myself during these periods of
reflection is: *Have I made a difference today?* Did I have an impact
on the young people who look to me for guidance? Is their world
a better place because of something I did or tried to do?

It is faith in God that helps my work stay alive with all the vigor
and energy I can muster to make a good impact on this and the
generations to follow.

God works in mysterious ways. In 1991, four 14 to 16 year olds
--Kevin, Monica, George, and Tamara -- asked for my guidance
to prepare them to move out on their own. As I thought of all
the challenges they would encounter and how ill prepared
they were, I knew in my heart that I had to somehow become
involved.

I became an "accidental director" and youth advocate. So with a
lot of inspiration, motivation, cooperation, dedication and
perspiration, I created Young Entrepreneurs of the Future, Inc.
(YEF) a 501 (c)(3) non-profit organization, founded to provide
youth with the necessary life skills to succeed in a competitive
society. This is accomplished through mentoring, coaching,
advocacy, hands-on-job training, and entrepreneurship.

264

We envision a future where economically disadvantaged youths accept personal responsibility for opening the door to opportunity when it knocks; doors fastened tight by poverty, lack of vision, or training. Our youth needs caring adults as mentors, coaches and advocates. As we work together, our program is a solid base from which our youth can grow and enrich the lives of all with whom they interact.

Helping the young grow up to be independent men and women takes proper training, and mental nourishing to produce respected and honored citizens. To do otherwise is to deprive them of what they have a right to expect; and to do wrong against the social institutions among which we all live.

YEF teaches the vital elements of entrepreneurship: goal setting, leadership development, time management and people skills. All donations go directly to scholarships for young people who need help. It also gives assistance to summer youth development programs.

Youth have the power so often inherent on youth, to see the world anew. My "pay-off" comes when a young girl or boy who did not believe they had a future when they came into our program, light up with joy and confidence, and exclaim: "I got it Miss Carolyn!". **We are all part of everthing and everyone.** It is up to us to live the vision and set the example. By starting where we are living in a spirit of love and giving and sharing, we create a, path of light for all God's children to enter the kingdom of Tomorrow.

* * *

Carolyn Stowers Harris
215-476-7659
YEF6027@msn.com
www.yefinc.org

Debra Ann Bartz

Captain Airline Pilot
Holistic Health Practitioner

Debra Ann Bartz

BIOGRAPHY

Debra Ann Bartz is a consummate advocate of changing the status quo by asking *"Why is it the way it is?"* When she did not find the right answer, she sought to expose the injustices even when up against authority figures.

As a graduate of the third class of women (1982) from the United States Air Force Academy, she graduated pilot training, sixth year of women (1983), and finally her dream became reality: **Debra Ann Bartz, Air Force Pilot!**

Once commissioned military officer and pilot, she found herself confronted with tremendously difficult times. She believed she had arrived at a place of "acceptance" as an equal. Far from it! From there she served twenty years in full and part-time capacities worldwide as an Air Force KC-135 Air Refueling Pilot, Air Operations Officer planning missions for the spy aircraft SR-71 missions.

After eight years of Air Force active duty (1990) and Masters of Science Human Resources Management, she continued her dream of flight by becoming a Commercial Airline Pilot - of which less than 5% of women were in flying commercial pilot ranks. Again, she thought she had arrived at a place of equal acceptance. Only six years earlier (1984) did she learn that all the airlines were sued by the EEOC (Equal Employment Opportunity Commission) to interview and hire women and other minorities. Once inside the ranks there was still more work to be done for full acceptance from those she worked with directly and indirectly.

Debra Ann Bartz has been honored with numerous accolades - to name but a few - Albert Nelson's Marquis Who's Who 2017 - 18, Lifetime Achievement Award featured in the Wall Street Journal December 4, 2018, Entrepreneur of the year 2015 in Holistic and Integrative Nutrition, Women of Distinction Magazine 8th edition, and the National Association of Women 2011-12 Woman of the Year.

DREAMS OF FLIGHT

by Debra Ann Bartz

"The courage it takes to share your story might be the very thing someone else needs to open their heart to hope."

Ever since I was ten years old (1970), I dreamt of becoming a commercial airline pilot. The inspiration took root while watching commercial jets flying over my hometown of Chicago, Illinois. Little did I know then the limitations of my dream of flight were set by the laws of society. As a child, I knew nothing about structural society laws. **Aren't laws meant to be challenged as we evolve and change?** Too many rules do not protect us, and instead bind us by limiting our beliefs in our personal power to control our own destiny.

So, dream I did! How would I go from dreams of flight to becoming a real-life pilot? In 1976, Congress passed a bill to open up access for women to the Military Service Academies and Undergraduate Pilot Training (UPT).

To take the steps necessary to even apply to, let alone be accepted and succeed in the military flight program, I first had to confront the many demons that needed reckoning on a personal level. I suffered from a really severe case of not "feeling good enough". I came from a large family, my parents both worked but we lived paycheck to paycheck. Growing up, I was exposed to great physical, emotional, and mental trauma doled out from both parents on a regular basis.

The more difficult life became for me, the more I escaped into dreams of flight. I knew I needed a mentor outside of my family. My desire was so profound I was able to find some adults who believed in me, and who assisted me in applying and being accepted to the Air Force Academy.

My survival instinct was and remains strong. I buried the trauma deep inside and mustered the strength to leave my abusive family for unknown challenges I would face at the nearly all male Air Force Academy in Colorado Springs.

Between the Air Force Academy and UPT, the hardest lesson to learn was that it did not matter how hard we worked or how much we achieved, as women we were still not given respect and recognition from the military echelons. Mentorship was scarce. I had to navigate the hidden path of fitting in while learning the rigors of becoming a military officer, earning a Bachelor of Science degree, and keeping my fitness levels up to be accepted for pilot training.

I began my military career at 18 years old and retired from the Air Force Reserves with 20 years of service at age 42; including a part time job with a major commercial airline at age 30. The years between entering the military to the commercial pilot ranks was very challenging to my personal life, since my professional life priorities of pursuing excellence and equality for women and minorities were my primary focus.

Children were my top priority professionally, if not personally, and I wanted to mentor young girls who were interested in pursuing non-traditional careers. I address these issues every opportunity I have with public speaking at grammar and high schools alike. *It was not until later after my military career was over that I settled into a mutually loving relationship of over 18 years so far.*

Life became a bit easier for women over time since there are more women pilots in the flying ranks. Consequently, we could reach out with mentorship programs through different non-profit organizations. I joined and served as an elected member for a six-year-term as treasurer; a two year-term board member, and a member of a scholarship committee during my tenure as a member of the Women Military Aviators www.womenmilitaryaviators.org an organization dedicated to historically preserving the stories of the pioneers who came before us.

Debra Ann Bartz

Even during the years leading up to the passing of the historic bill allowing women to serve in combat 1993-1994, this organization was instrumental in helping overturn the combat exclusion law. I testified as a member-at large to a group of civilians reporting directly to the President of the Unitd States, called the Defense Advisory Committee of Women in the Services (D.A.C.O.W.I.T.S).

After flying for 20 years for a major airline, my health began to unravel. My disorder became a concern that threatened my flying career. This became another major concern for me, as I was not prepared to deal with the monstrous system of the Federal Aviation Administration(FAA) and the traditional medical system. The FAA would only look at the traditional medical system of treatment to manage an illness. So without much health knowledge, I accepted the diagnosis and remedies so I could return to flying; but not without waivers and the threat of a possible unrelated illness due to the side effects of the drug I was prescribed.

So I bucked the system again and earned my American Association of Drugless Practitioner (A.A.D.P.) Board Certified Holistic Health Practitioner in Nutrition and other certifications to educate myself and others in disease prevention; all the while starting my health and wellness home-based business called **Learn Conquer Soar Coaching.** With this knowledge, I got off all the drugs and fly without any waivers that could have threatened my Captain Airline Pilot status.

Now, in addition to my airline pilot career, I became a health advocate. I find myself counselling those I fly with - who may well become future clients. Mentoring and education are so important to share with each other in this ever-changing world so dependent on human relationships.

Lessons Learned

The ones that stand out the most for me is to accept every opportunity presented to assist others through mentorship, and increase the understanding that you can live with integrity and it's still okay to "buck the system". I feel I influence future generations of girls as an Air Force Academy Liaison Officer by interviewing and visiting grammar schools and high schools, as a member of the Women Military Aviators, Women in Aviation and Girls in Aviation volunteer at United Airlines. I do that by mentoring and removing some of the mystery of what it takes for a woman to become a pilot.

It is within our power to change the stories of our past and rewrite the limiting beliefs we may have carried forward. I'd like to serve as an example for other women struggling with self-worth due to childhood traumas and help change minds on societal gender issues. I think it's very important for girls and young women in our rapidly changing world to profit from one another's experience, and to have role models they can look up to with pride.

Life sometimes is not fair, but opportunities are abundant if you pursue excellence in all you do. Personal and professional relationships are a must to get ahead, which otherwise can stall your progress if insisting on travelling your journey alone. Health, too, is taken for granted at times while going for your goals. I urge all to resist soul-wrenching pressures by acknowledging the reality of your true nature. Let your dreams take flight! *Dreams do come true!*

* * *

Debra Ann Bartz
www.learnconquersoarcoaching.com
www.debrabartz.com
www.coachdebra.bemergroup.com

Tonja Demoff

Wealth Strategist
Speaker, Consultant

Tonja Demoff

BIOGRAPHY

Tonja Demoff is a multi-published author and speaker who loves to teach and inspire others to greater heights. Her popular titles include *FRESH START; The Resilient Millionaire; Twist & Trust; CORE Wealth; The Entrepreneur's Edge ; The Casual Millionaire : Wealth by Intention;Bubble Proof:Real Estate Strategies That Work in any Market; Millionaire Mindset; Believe and Achieve; Commission Checks : How to Close More Deals & Deposit more Income.*

As a trainer, teacher, consultant, and real estate agent/investment guru, Tonja knows the highs and lows of entrepreneurial life, She uses that knowledge to help others create their own fresh starts and to develop the entrepreneur's edge to enjoy more lasting and sustaining highs.

Tonja has decades of experience running businesses and incredibly popular seminars. Tonja's students learn business principles AND master their mindset- so they make money and keep it. Entrepreneurs in the field of real estate and ALL fields learn from her expertise and appreciate her candor, wit, and intelligence.

Her popular seminars teach strategy and mindset, the powerful combination of true and lasting success. Clients are able to learn the mechanics of making money and how to maintain the proper mindset to hold on to their wealth.

Tonja continues to create programs to serve her clients who want to succeed in business - any kind of business - for the long haul. Tonja loves to teach, to connect, and to share the principles that lead to a life of prosperity and vitality.

Traveling the world for business and pleasure, Tonja operates her companies out of California and Texas. She is also a member of the United States Air Force.

A FRESH START

How to bounce back from pain and struggle and live an amazing life!

by Tonja Demoff

"Life never presents us with anything which may not be looked upon as a fresh starting point." ~Andre Gide

What do I know about making a fresh start? **Plenty!** I've had more than a few in my life. One example is being sued by a former friend and business partner. A few years ago, I was involved in a very lengthy lawsuit and ended up filing for bankruptcy.

I know the pain of losing money and fighting off the feeling of humiliation. There were times when it was so easy to point the finger of blame. Holding on to my anger seemed to hold me together. I knew I had done nothing wrong and yet staying in the energy of spite and revenge did nothing to speed up the trial process or repair neither the damage to our relationship nor my bank account.

Getting sued was like a punch in the gut. Her attempts to ruin my reputation were so hurtful. My biggest fear had always been about other people's perception of me. What they thought of me mattered. Here I was being accused of being a fraud. The terror!

My reputation mattered to me (and yes, it still does), but now I no longer harbor the fear. I KNOW that I can come through anything because of WHO I AM. Being in fear of what people think of me is no longer an issue because I faced the worst, and I'm still standing, stronger than ever. No one or nothing can "ruin" me and they can't you either.

When I came out of my lawsuit, I had to regroup. I had to pull back and stop blaming. I had to stop spinning in cycles of "I was wronged. This is so unfair!" I had to do my mindset work: I had to make my Fresh Start.

Think about the word "fresh" and all the images it conjures in your mind. A new beginning. A fresh face. A fresh new day. Something deliciously fresh from the oven. Fresh vegetables straight from the farmer's market. Minty fresh. What do you come up with when you think of the word fresh?

The online dictionary merriam-webster.com gives a definition of fresh as "newly produced, gathered, or made, not frozen or canned." Another meaning is pure and clean. A Fresh Start is to be washed off and let the old troubles be flushed away. How to do that? Think some newly produced thoughts! We get to gather them! We get to make them!

We often go through life as automatic robots. We have been programmed to operate in a certain way. We often feel frozen, trapped, stuck in the rut of the daily grind. Merriam-webster.com goes on to give full definition that states fresh means "having its original qualities unimpaired; full of or renewed in vigor."

The Fresh Start is returning you to the knowing of your "original qualities unimpaired." We humans are energetic beings. We are energy, pure and clean. A Fresh Start gets you back to that understanding. Your original qualities are that of pure power and full potential.

Your ability to wield your power has been impaired by society, schooling, and the system. We are born knowing that we are capable beings, yet as we grow up, and starting when we are very young, we are taught that we are powerless. We are taught to be fearful. To return to our true state is the best fresh start ever.

A Fresh Start is knowing that I am the one in charge of my life. No lawsuit, no betrayal, no loss of money can change who I am. Nothing that happens in your life can change the reality of who you are. No matter what has happened, you can implement a new beginning: it can change the trajectory of your life. Challenges are opportunities that grow and enhance our lives and our perception. I now know that I could get hit with a lawsuit, a disease, or a natural disaster and it does not change who I am. I am more than what I thought I lost. I am energy, pure and clean. Always.

The decision to make a Fresh Start can happen instantly. You must decide that you no longer want to feel helpless or powerless or overwhelmed. You also have to decide that you no longer want to carry around bitterness, resentment, or anger.

This mindset work is also like a course in stress reduction. You begin to see that the world is not out to get to you. You do not have to live in fear. You do not have to live in worry. You are energy, pure and clean, full of power and potential. You can make a Fresh Start every day. Start today.

To create your own Fresh Start, follow these steps from my book : *FRESH START.*

Permission: Give yourself permission to rant and rave and whine and moan. Throw yourself on the floor and wall. Beat up your pillow. Scream and shout and cry until you are exhausted.

Accept: Accept what happened. It is a done deal. There is no going back. There are no do-overs. Do not replay the reel in your mind over and over again. Release blame. This work is invinsible, and not always easy, but it is so worth it.

Release: Release the need for "answers." Let go of having to know why something happened. We spend a lot of fruitless time asking the heavens, "Why did this happen to me? Why? Why?" Let. It. Go.

Affirm: Write and say these statements in your head and out loud every day and every night. "NOTHING can change who I am. I AM MORE than what I thought I lost. NOTHING CAN CHANGE WHO I AM. I AM MORE THAN WHAT I THOUGHT I LOST."

Reflect: Step back and become the impartial observer. This can be difficult at first, but keep at it. From a bird's eye view, look at your situation with no emotion. Ask yourself: What did I learn? What is my take-away from this event? Where do I go from here?

Gratitude: As hard it may seem sometimes, there is always something to be grateful for. My lawsuit mess became the impetus for several books and seminars. My work now is inspired because of all that I have been through. I now serve at an even deeper level because of my lessons learned. Gratitude is one of the most powerful forces in this life. Harness the wave of appreciation.

Visualize: You get to make up your own mind. You are the creator of your life. Visualize how you want your life to be going forward. Take a few minutes every morning to imagine what you want for yourself. And then allow it to come to you!

In my book, *FRESH START,* I share my own stories of overcoming challenges like bankruptcy, betrayal, and loss of friendship, and I relate stories and examples of clients and students. I also break down how to do the work - the inner work - to create a Fresh Start no matter what has happened to you. Following the simple steps can change your life!

* * *

Tonja Demoff
(562)266-6390
www.virtualreconsulting.com

Jory H. Fisher, JD, PCC

Speaker, Business Coach
Sales & Communications Trainer

Jory H. Fisher, JD, PCC

BIOGRAPHY

Jory Fisher has enjoyed a diverse career in government, law, education, and entrepreneurship. As an attorney in Virginia for nearly 30 years, Jory focused on cases involving child abuse and neglect, juvenile delinquency, and domestic relations. She also served as a founding faculty member of Liberty University School of Law and Associate Dean for Career & Professional Development.

In 2008, Jory launched her business as a professionally certified coach. Although she was thrilled to work from home and attend more of her children's activities, she grappled with questions like: How do I attract clients? How much do I charge? What's the best use of my resources? How do I run a fulfilling, *profitable* business? She emerged as a passionate business coach and communications trainer for small business owners and sales professionals who want to make a bigger, more meaningful difference in the world – *and* more money.

Jory's coaching and training credentials include Professional Certified Coach, Master Certified Christian Coach, Certified Career Management Coach, Certified Business Coach & Startup Expert, and Certified Trainer of the BANKCODE methodology. She serves as Executive Director of Admissions for BLU University, an online learning community for entrepreneurs, and as the host and organizer of several Meetup groups in Baltimore, MD.

Jory graduated Phi Beta Kappa, *summa cum laude* from Southern Methodist University. She earned her Master's degree in Spanish from Middlebury College and her law degree from the University of Virginia.

In 2012, after raising a blended family of seven children, Jory and her husband Dave moved from Lynchburg, VA to Bel Air, MD. Jory's interests include faith, family, fitness, therapeutic horseback riding, adult congenital heart disease, and muscular sclerosis.

Jory H. Fisher, JD, PCC

Are You a High-Quality Leader?

Values, Vision and Personality Traits

by Jory Fisher

"We're all leaders. The question is: what kind of leader are we?"

History is replete with women leaders whose Values, Vision, and Personality Traits cause them to stand out as women we admire and wish to emulate. We're *all* leaders. The question is: what kind of leader are we?

Throughout the centuries, women (and men of course) have misused their influence for more power, more prestige, and more possessions. When choosing which leaders to follow or which leaders to invite to join us on a mission or project, we must look at the person's Values, Vision, and Personality Traits. Similarly, when discerning whether we would be a good fit for a leadership role, we are wise to consider our own Values, Vision, and Personality Traits. If we see a red flag (a mis-fit) with *any* of those factors, we could be faced with a challenge right away or with a full-blown problem down the road. It's better to pause and make a sound, well-informed decision now than regret our decision later.

We can learn a lot about ourselves by taking online personality assessments. Like many of you, I've taken several. I'm aware of my strengths, weaknesses, spiritual gifts, likes, dislikes, and buying behavior. I'm "leadership material" according to the assessments. I like leading, provided the cause is one I believe in wholeheartedly and the people are fun to work with.

What about you? According to assessments you've taken or comments you've received, are you naturally a leader? Do you enjoy leading? Suppose you get to choose a project to work on for the next eight hours, or eight months, would you be happy if most of your responsibilities required the skills and talents of a leader?

280

If you wish to be a *high-quality* leader, I invite you to answer the following questions to discern the kind of leader you wish to be, the type of leadership you wish to provide, and the types of causes you're here on earth to advocate for, promote, and/or support.

1. What has given you a sense of accomplishment and fulfillment during school, work, or leisure time?

2. What kind of needs, problems, and issues concern you? What keeps you awake at night? What articles do you read? Look at your whole life, e.g., your work, volunteer activities, and hobbies.

3. If you could do what you really wanted, what would you do? What is in your heart? What do you think would give you the most joy?

4. List and then rank your Knowledge, Strengths, Skills, Gifts, and Abilities. Look back over all your experiences—education, career, volunteer work, leisure activities, etc. What do you know or do well?

5. List, then rank, the values you hold near to your heart. Consider what you deem important, what gives meaning to your life and work, what compels you to action, and what defines your fundamental character.

6. Which individuals or groups pull at your heartstrings? Whom do you feel called to serve? Why? What is it about those individuals or groups that makes you want to reach out to them? What pain do you want to ease? What problem do you long to solve?

7. What other clues do you see in your life journey that might indicate the kind of leader you're called to be? For example, what pain have you experienced? What lessons have you learned? What losses and failures have helped you become the person you are today?

America needs high-quality women leaders! The questions above can serve as an excellent foundation for your role as a high-quality leader at home, at work, in your community, and in the marketplace.

Speaking of home... there's nothing more important than how we model leadership as spouses and parents. I'm proud to say my six grown daughters and stepdaughters are now leading strongly and bravely in their respective industries (science, education, languages, entrepreneurship, theatre & film, and the U.S. Navy). They've stepped out into the world in a big way, doing what they're designed to do.

I'd like to add a few more ingredients to this recipe for leadership success. We must: * Recognize our weakness and get help to overcome them. * Be transparent about our challenges and shortcomings. * Have a sense of humor!!

I am WAY more inclined to follow someone who recognizes her weaknesses, is transparent about her "opportunities for growth," and laughs about her imperfections. That is, I'd MUCH rather learn from someone (and be someone) who light-heartedly admits her soufflés have fallen than someone who brags that her soufflés turn out beautifully all the time.

We do not have to be perfect to be high-quality leaders! We "just" need to be willing to become the high-quality leaders we're called to be and do the work to make that happen. I'd love to hear one action step you're choosing to take today and why that action step is important to you. Bless you as you proceed upon your leadership journey

* * *

Jory H. Fisher, JD, PCC
jory@joryfisher.com
434.258.6793
www.joryfisher.com

Ortell Diane Cromer

Founder/Owner
Diane Cromer Enterprises

Ortell Diane Cromer

BIOGRAPHY

Diane Cromer has enjoyed a successful forty-year career working on four continents leading, consulting, and teaching teams engaged in political campaigns, issues and advocacy advancement and organizational development. Her professional focus is strategic and public communications. Starting in broadcast journalism covering politics for ABC affiliates in Pittsburgh and Philadelphia, Diane has spent the past 20 years working with countries and companies transitioning from communist economies to market economies and from dictatorships to democracy. The mid-portion of her career was devoted to domestic political consulting servicing as research, media and general consult for candidates. Diane has had a decision-making role at every electoral level from local to state to federal.

She has been an instructor of business communications and public speaking at University of Maryland's R.H. Smith School of Business MBA program and taught elements of campaigning at the Yale Campaign School for Women, the Pennsylvania Women's Campaign Schools at Chatham and Shippensburg Universities, the Democratic National Committee and the AMA.

She also developed and led educational programs for adults and youth in Eastern Europe, South East Asia, the Middle East and Africa for the National Democratic Institute of International Affairs, the United Nations Development Program, and individual USAID programs. In 2007-2014, she found the Cromer Group, a company in Serbia, specializing in the work-place skills and career counseling needed by a young population that had never before had the opportunity to plan and prepare for career choices or the need for lifelong learning.

She holds an MBA from the University of Liverpool, England having received top honors. Her work has been recognized in 1990 in Who's Who of Women Executives, named a "Rising Star" by *Campaigns and Elections Magazine* in 1998, and was the Lebanon Valley (PA) Chamber of Commerce's 1999 Athena Award recipient. Most recently, Diane was selected for the 2008-2009 Presidential Who's Who among business and professional achievers in the United States.

Good Communications drives Good Results

by Ortell Diane Cromer

"Be quiet, listen, think ... then, communicate to open hearts and minds and to champion possibilities."

In August 2000, I sat on the banks of the Danube as a blazing sun set behind the ancient city of Pest. That evening closed six months of consulting and training for the coalition of Serbian leaders working to end Slobodan Milosevic's authoritarian rule. The six-week election would begin the following day.

How did a kid who grew up in the 1950s and '60s from a Pennsylvania farming community of 750 find herself in Hungary teaching people to fight for free elections and economic opportunity -- people brave enough to spend a decade of poverty enduring continuous harassment, searches of home and offices and even jail? As one of several nationally recognized consultants sent in 2000 by the Clinton administration to deliver test trainings to Serbia's opposition leadership, I was chosen by the group to serve as the coalition's consultant. **Why?**

Educated in Yale, Cambridge, the Sorbonne and Harvard, these Serbian leaders moved among their contemporaries in Washington, D.C., and Brussels, Belgium. They loved being with consultants from presidential races and loved the stories more. But that was not my experience. As owner of one of the earliest wholly female-owned political consulting firms in Washington, D.C., I worked on races labeled as unwinnable. My stories were of women engaged in elections where community and party structures worked together to protect the status quo. Most needed to learn everything about campaigns and how to win with too little of everything; 63 percent of them did.

My stories are nuts and bolts--the things you want to take notes on, not the tales told over beer into the night.

I asked questions. And more questions. The picture of their reality began to unfold. They were stuck on trying to figure out how to get what they didn't have - and could never get. They were under threat by entrenched power that wanted to keep it that way. International bodies labeled the race unwinnable. They had too little of everything. They saw three elections stolen because they could not protect their vote. **I became a lead consultant for the coalition that defeated Milosevic because I listened**. I heard them. What I had to say to them was what they needed to hear - how to leverage what they had to build what they needed for a winning coalition, and, they were the women and men who could do it. Their historic victory has been retold on film, in video, books and newspapers and studied at universities.

Test Yourself and Your Ideas

Communications is my passion. It is a way to coach people from one tightly held thought to new ideas that can solve problems or change outmoded behaviors. The words persuade, convince and explain have no place when talking about communications. Discourse is best served when people own their ideas.

Communications' job is to understand people and appreciate their goals. I started putting that theory together in my teens and knew I wanted to test it professionally. Fourteen years into my career, I was frustrated at remaining the number two person in the office, earning half my male predecessor's salary and being unable to test my emerging ideas for better communications. That combination drove me to launch my company in1987. I firmly believed that real communications is achieved through aligning the goals of an audience and the goals of a client. That philosophy has sustained DCE for 30 years.

Only You Can Decide To Quit

Like most women in this publication, I endured endless slights and worse. My first reality was being rejected from the Little League. Despite being one of the 10 best players in the field, I was a girl. Disappointed but resolute that I was competent, I negotiated to serve as a warm-up catcher. Twenty years later, while creating an educational video for a client, I had a unique idea for animation, a challenge in 1984. My video experience and study of animation suggested it was doable. The male production team, echoing the tones of the Little League coaches, told me I would fail. I was willing to take the risk but needed their commitment to help me be successful. That video served my client well; the studio ultimately used it on their demo reel.

Failure or embarrassment is not pleasant. But neither defined me or my work. They are steps to new skills and opportunities. External pressures can be difficult and demanding. To continue, or to change or say "this is not the right time or it's not the path to follow" is entirely OK, as long as it is our choice.

* * *

Diane Cromer
TheCromerCompany@gmail.com
(202)285-0211

Dr. Marium Murad, MD

International Health Expert

President & Founder
Movement Is Blessed LLC

Dr. Marium Murad

BIOGRAPHY

Dr. Marium Murad, Founder of **'Movement Is Blessed'**©, is recognized internationally for 25 years as a pioneer in developing a natural exercise program, which emphasizes utilizing the body's natural motion for health and harmony. Originally made for her mother. *"Her work is brilliant, she is gracious, kind hearted, and inspirational. Her intellectual rigor, perseverance and passion for helping people is exceptional."* (IAOTP)

After graduating Fatima Jinnah Medical College, Dr. Murad marries her fiancé in the petroleum industry, and while living internationally, she specializes in east/west, traditional/cultural, new/old techniques of healthy living, healing, aging and longevity. This broad spectrum of A to Z global remedies provides the robust foundation for her program, which soars to extraordinary heights in a very short time. *"Dr. Murad's work has worldwide recognition for her continuous commitment and dedication to making a difference in the daily life of the average person."* (Continental Who's Who)

A 2014 New Year's launch for the MB Program. In 2014 Dr. Murad is named **VIP Woman of the Year** by the National Association of Professional Women. In 2015 **Top Female Executive** and 2016 **Delegate** by International Women's Leadership Association. In 2016-2017 **Top Healthcare Leader of the Year** by International Association of Top Professionals (IAOTP). In 2017 **Empowered Entrepreneurial Woman** by CUTV News. **Member of the Year** by International Society of Business Leaders. **Top Ten Women of the Year** by Women of Distinction. **Top Ten Doctors of the Year** by Strathmore Worldwide Who's Who. **Best in Medicine** by the American Health Council. **Professional Women** by Who's Who.com. **Marquis Top Doctor** by Marquis Who's Who. **Elite American Physician** by Worldwide Branding. **Top Female Professional** by Universal Publishing Corporation. 2019 **Woman of the Year** by International Who's Who.

Dr. Murad attributes her success to following her beloved parent's footsteps. Future plans are to introduce daily exercise to every household worldwide, and open a foundation for handicapped children, providing treatment and education to become future doctors.

Life is Movement, Movement is Life, and Movement Is Blessed©

by Dr. Marium Murad, MD

Like many families, my story starts at home, I cannot be thankful enough for having the best and friendliest parents possible. It's not just me saying this, my whole school, my friends and the neighbors think so too.

> *"Mom's your first friend, best friend and forever friend."*
> *— Arabic Quote*

This quote speaks for all of us that are fortunate to be blessed with parents, who encourage us and believe in ourselves. Their love paves the way for us to explore the miracle-making powers that lay dormant within us. I clearly understand, at a very early age that I must meet a rigorous set of high standards that will never be lowered to make it easy for me. I accept at a young age that I could do anything and, with this fact, my confidence within myself grew.

> *"High expectations are the key to everything."*
> *— N. Walton*

Parental attitude is extremely important in shaping a child's future. Children are natural imitators. We are born to instinctively trust our parents, and through our parents influence, learn to trust ourselves. You may tell a child one hundred times a day to smile but, if he sees a frown on the parent's face, that is the expression the child will unconsciously imitate. Words alone are not enough, but set a good example, that is the lesson the child will unconsciously imitate your every move.

> *"The best kind of parent you can be, is to lead by example."*
> *— D. Barrymore*

My parent's best gift to me, an encouraging message, "My child, I believe in you" This message still radiates within me, giving me confidence to soar high and to become a way of life that naturally leads to desires and dreams coming true.

"The goal of education is the advancement of knowledge and the dissemination of truth." - President John Kennedy

The real reason behind my success is the love and support of my parents who taught me to be all that I can be. If I want it, I can do it. I must try, and when I try, I'll achieve it, despite obstacles or challenges in the path. It all begins with believing in yourself, and using your knowledge in service of yourself and others.

The answer, follow your deepest dreams, at times the path isn't clearly visible or defined. You may choose a path less travelled on, or may clear bushes, where no path exists. Follow your instincts, remember your parent's guidance. In any situation, do what you feel is best for yourself and in service of others.

Your goal is worth the time, worth the effort and worth the sacrifice. Following your dreams, your heart's passion, life's full time work and sometimes you have to work at it until it hurts. It doesn't come easy and it definately doesn't come overnight.

"Intelligence plus character, that is the true goal of education."
– Dr. Martin Luther King

My life's journey is cemented with experiences of my parents, helping others, but true help starts from home, with my beloved family. We're an arthritic family, that's a titanic load in itself to state briefly in a sentence. One of my earliest memories is of my awesome grandmother.

"If nothing is going well, call your grandma."
– Italian Proverb

I remember with excitement when I heard my blessed Mom say: "Guess what! Grandma's coming to visit."

Grandma's always happy to see me, beaming a huge ear-to-ear smile. Grandma's all about hugs and kisses. I love grandma's visits, it's fun, Grandma brings me lots of gifts, and on top of that Grandma buys me anything I mention I like.

> *"Between the earth and the sky above, nothing can match a grandmother's love." – Asian Saying.*

Coming from an arthritic family, my grandma walks using a walker, and her knees look like two small hard balls. She walks rather slowly, dragging one foot forwards, stops momentarily for a pause to catch her breath. Then, continues in slow-motion to lift the other foot up very slightly off the ground, to slowly drag the other foot forwards. Grandma's knees don't straighten but she manages to be self-mobile, with her walker.

She's cheerful conversation anytime, grandma never tires of telling her delightful, favorite family stories. My Grandma's mind is alert and heart content, however her arthritic hands and knees tell a different physical reality. Now looking back, I'm sure grandma's knees hurt really badly but she never complained. Sending Grandma heavenly love.

> *"Words that will change your life. You have arthritis."*
> *– Arthritis Foundation*

As far as I can remember, my sweet mom's knees made her appear physically slow even through my mother's a woman of action. Come medicine time, one of us kids gets mom's medicine from the kitchen cabinet. Living with swollen, stiff knees is not easy.

My mother's a wonderful woman with noble traits, my rock, and my role model. Mom's active at home, in the neighborhood, at community events, at school, and above all I never heard my mother use the word, "No". Absolutely cherish mom, value her opinion and I follow her advice.

"Gild pure gold, but not possible to make mom more beautiful."
– Gandhi

One day, soon after I join medical college, a brilliant idea dawns upon me, a method to help my mother's arthritic knees. I quickly assemble my thoughts onto paper. To my utter amazement, my mother's life changes drastically. Mom finds my knee program like a God send miracle, she's been praying to happen for her rather sore and stiff knees. My mother's super excited, super thrilled and over joyous, telling everyone in sight of her daughter's knee program as mom's getting phenomenal results.

"Being able to walk pain-free is a blessing. Being able to walk without showing pain is a skill." *– K. McPherson*

Any person my mother knows to have the slightest knee ailment, is my mom's student, learning my knee program from her. Miraculously everyone experiences healing results and my knee program is an instant hit. Everyone wants to book a follow-up appointment with me, at my clinic. They're shocked to learn, I'm only a first year medical student and not a full doctor. All praise mom for her help and tell her, "Your daughter will be a famous doctor. She has healing hands and definitely inform us when she starts her clinic."

"If one way be better than another, that you may be sure is . . . Nature's way." *– Aristotle*

My mother's extremely proud of me and I'm ecstatic to see mom jubilant. Soon after, one day mom tells me that my knee program is giving her the same results as her medicine. Mom's been taking her arthritic medicine for decades and suffers from a stomach ulcer, a common complication as arthritic medicine wasn't buffer coated then. Mom decides to continue with my knee program and stops taking her ulcer causing medicine.

"Good health and good sense are two of life's greatest blessings."
– Syrus

My life is heaven, fortunate of live a precious life, being raised by my caring and loving parents. Not a wish in my heart that isn't fulfilled.

Then, one day, unexpectedly my dear father. . . my executive father from his work stress, travel stress, and his other stresses I never knew, suffers a heart attack. He's only 54, and it proves fatal ... he's gone. My father, my constant source of encouragement, my pillar of support was gone. I remember my father as a very caring man, soft spoken, never angry, and he loved spending time with us.

The years that follow are emotionally draining, especially for my mother. Being widowed at a young age; devastated by losing her loving husband and her soul mate. Over time, my mother's health continues to slowly decline. Then suddenly one day, my mother's health takes a severe downward plunge and mom's hospitalized, and put on complete bed rest. The prognosis isn't favorable and things are not looking good.

"You have to be your strongest, when you are feeling your weakest."
– Unknown

I rush back home, what I see sends a shiver down my spine, my dearly beloved mother lying motionless in bed, heavily sedated, eyes closed, barely alive. As a medical doctor, I understand the medical language doctor's use, I understand beyond the doctor's conversations, and I understand the doctor's instructions on what the patients needs. I know mom's a complicated patient taking loads of medicine for her list of health conditions, which she developed over the past decade, since Dad rose to heaven.

"Love is the ring, and the ring has no end."
– French Proverb

The next few days are crucial, my mother has a weak heart, lying motionless is hazardous for her heart, whereas movement is not possible for a bad back. At my mother's bedside, in an effort to address multiple conflicting, serious health concerns simultaneously,

I assemble a unique blend of medical and alternatives, in an urgent effort to formulate a functional remedy, with no time for trial and error. At my mother's bedside, **'Movement Is Blessed'**© takes form.

"When life gets harder, challenge yourself to be stronger."
– Russian Proverb

Thankfully, mom recovers completely, even her doctors are surprised at her speedy recovery. This was over twenty years ago. Since then, I've helped tons of people worldwide with my remarkable natural exercise technique.

Movement Is Blessed© Philosophy:

Movement Creates and Sustains Life

All life begins with movement and motion. Whether you look at the Big-Bang creating the universe, or look into the origin of man. The very moment of creation involves movement, active movement. And when all movement stops, life stops. In other words, when all movement and all motion cease, life ceases. All of our body systems begin to shut down, and life cannot continue to exist.

For all life to survive, movement is required. For our existence, movement is required. Movement is essential, movement is absolutely crucial, and we must move at all costs. Whatever it takes, then why do most of us, don't have a few minutes to spare for ourselves. Majority of people invest time to fly high soaring mental kites in their weekly planners, without corresponding time for any physical activity in their daily lives.

"Life requires movement."
– Aristotle

Why do most of us, not exist with sufficient responsibility in our lives? Why do we not give ourselves enough self-worth to spend a few minutes of the 24 hours on our well-being? When will we learn this life lesson of great value?

"It's not about having time, it's about making time.
– R. Bermingham

Thousands of years ago, ancient civilizations knew the worth of physical activity. Their wise men were preaching and coaching that life requires movement. A little movement goes a long way. In fact, you are moving unconsciously, at this very moment in time and space. At this very second, your internal body is in continuous motion. Not only is your internal body in continuous movement mode at this very second, your internal body has been and remains in constant motion since the day you were born. Our bodies have their own internal rhythmic movements. At all times the heart beats and a ripple movement spreads through the whole body.

"Nothing happens until you move."
– Einstein

Stillness is not good, being physically motionless is not good for anyone, at any age, and at any time. Being still burdens our physical body and burdens our mental acuity. A healthy body moves. The modern sedentary lifestyle is not desirable for any individual. Limited physical motion leads to rapid deterioration in health.

"He who would move mountains, move yourself first."
– Socrates

What can you do for yourself? Yes, we all know that daily exercise is good for us, but only a small percentage of health enthusiast go to the gym regularly. Statistically, we're a health conscious nation. Every household has 2-3 fitness gadgets, 5-6 health books and a kitchen cabinet full of supplements. Plus a steady supply of marketing flyers to remind us to buy more.

"Be kind, everyone is fighting their own battles."
– Plato

A vibrant life, great health, overall wellness, and being physically fit, represents an intricately interwoven matrix, representing different sides of a cube. It may appear to be manually adjustable, but a little tug and pull will prove its point of unified existence. You'll see that the bonds are strong, yes stronger, as they interconnect at multiple levels. Finely interlinked that it's a task, to have one without the other.

The same analogy holds true for our physical body which is inter-linked with our internal body organs, which in turn is very closely inter-connected with our mind. Each strengthens the other when physical activity is in place. However, each weakens the other if we are physically inactive.

This powerful statement by President Kennedy proves that in the 1960's the concept of 'mind, body, soul,' exists then, which is the catch phrase today. Start anywhere, you'll gain external and internal body health via physical activity.

"Physical fitness is not only one of the most important keys to a healthy body. It's the basis of dynamic and creative intellectual activity."
- President Kennedy

Movement Is Blessed© Introduction

Daily Exercise for Everyone Everyday

My program's purpose is to directly teach you, what you can do for yourself. Empower you, enable you, without any dependency on anyone to take better care of yourself. Understand a few wellness principles, and apply them on yourself. Teach you easy, economical, yet effective steps of self- care. Make daily excercise a part of your everyday life. It's not the milestones that count but the daily small steps that pave the way by cementing the building blocks, leading to your larger goal.

"He who takes care of his body, takes care of his house."
– Plato

I explain using simple language for an example of a house. The walls and roof stand on a foundation, a solid sturdy foundation. You hire the best expert builder, specializing in construction, to lay the foundation for your house. The experienced, specialist designs to expertly build the foundation. The house's foundation supports this house, for as long as the house stands.

"Our soul dwells in our body, and our body resides in our house."
– Dalai Lama

But what about your body's foundation? Your body's foundation is the most neglected part of the body. Do we look at our body's foundation? Do we think of our body's foundation? Do we put in daily effort to maintain the wellness of our body's foundation? A vast majority cannot even reach or touch their feet!

"Out of sight, out of mind."
– English Saying

My speciality, expert natural wellness; I teach children, women, men, and seniors to be healthy, to be active and independently live at home. We love our houses, we live in them, we decorate and we remodel them. The house captures our hearts and our souls. A house as an example, better explains the similarities between the body and the house.

"I love my house. I love my family. I love my pets."
– J. King

As we stay busy in the cities hustle and bustle, relying on our foundation, and it's the condition of our foundation that we stand on. Yet statistically, it's the most neglected part of our body.

My purpose is to teach you, how to strengthen your body's foundation. All you need is a little daily exercise, and voila, you're independent and freely mobile. Walk where your heart desires, walk in the house, or walk in the park. No one wants to live a dependent life. The deciding factor is not your age or the condition of your mind, the deciding factor is the condition of your body's foundation; walking or wheelchair?

"At worst, a house un-kept cannot be as distressing as a life unlived."
— R. Macaulay

Like they say, everything's larger in Texas, return back home, seems like a buy-one-get-one-free sale going on. In Texas, everything and everyone's larger in size. Statistically Texas is #50th adult's insured state, that's not healthy, but Texas is economically strong, thankfully Texas is an ethnic state where families live together.

"My house is not a place, it's a people."
— Lois Bujold

Live-in Texan parents take care of all household chores; cleaning, cooking, laundry, babysitting, while young Texans work all day to come home and relax, carefree. Clean house, food cooked, kids in bed, all's done for you, today and every day, love sake.

"Women are the largest untapped reservoir of talent in this world."
— Hillary Clinton

One fact of Texas that surprises me is that Texas, officially has seven languages. I'm translating my program into all seven languages and Braille. Teach parents how to take care of themselves at home. Keep both Texas and grandma healthy.

"Everywhere immigrants have enriched and strengthened the fabric of American Life." — President John Kennedy

SCIENCE-BASED TOEZERCISE

As a Medical Doctor, trained in both western and alternative medicine, I'm deeply honored, truly blessed to re-invent the concept of daily exercise, while upholding the Principles of Human Body Science and Exercise Science. Now, allow me to introduce **TOEZERCISE**, the one exercise that's a workout.

"Let's examine the facts: daily exercise is required by everyone every day, but not everyone exercises every day." For a large number of us with a job, its lack of time or too tired from work overload. For an even larger number of us, we have no way to go to the gym, or invest in gym-wear with fit bits and shy away from personal trainers, or what people at the gym might say or think of us. To make a long story short, make exercise safe and to satisfy all excuses remotely possible.

TOEZERCISE: ONE Exercise Workout. Let's all try this jam-pack tiny giant, fully functional daily exercise, at your convenience, anytime, anyplace, without anything or anyone. Suitable for everyone alive with multiple benefits of an exercise workout.

A special, all-natural formulation, an effective ultimate luxury loaded daily exercise, which works wonders for its users, regardless of age and ability, reinforces confidence, and reinstates daily physical activity into the lives of each one of us. No two days are alike and a week, a month or a year... This all natural alternative is for you to super charge yourself in minutes-a-day, today and every day. Try this unique exercise experience today and become addicted to daily exercise.

"The only source of knowledge is experience."
– Einstein

At first glance, **TOEZERCISE** sounds totally insignificant with a bizarre twist, but a closer look, tremendously increases interest in **TOEZERCISE** which strengthens the body's foundation. This wellness tool is a master piece, and will soon be a household name, worldwide.

"The art of medicine consists of amusing the patient,
while nature cures the disease." – Voltaire

WELCOME COLLABORATION

I personally extend a friendly invite to each one of you, allow us to show you, how your life will change with this natural wonder of a daily convenient exercise for less active days from any reason. Just remember its not vertical age, it's the broad breath of national inactivity of a sedentary American lifestyle.

Each physical human body, regardless of age, requires daily exercise. **TOEZERCISE** especially for last trimester pregnant moms, toddlers, school kids, teens, young adults, middle age, mature ages, baby boomers and the elderly seniors.

An open invitation to all small or large associations, organizations, institutions, and companies. Try **TOEZERCISE** for **Executive / Employee Wellness Programs and Events.** Easy add-on to a meeting or event as a flexible, educational format, a short talk, quick demo to a full keynote or all-day workshop!

My work is, and has been to plant positive seeds in individuals, in families, and in communities worldwide. We need to collaborate together, thrive as a nation and as a global community. Let us, Leading Ladies, affirm our friendship on a networking platform to provide educational tools and personal inspiration, necessary for the next generation to become the Leaders of Tomorrow.

* * *

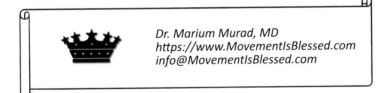

Dr. Marium Murad, MD
https://www.MovementIsBlessed.com
info@MovementIsBlessed.com

Cindy Galvin

International Leadership Developer

Rewiring the Brain through Neuroscience

Cindy Galvin

BIOGRAPHY

Cindy Galvin is a keynote speaker, non-executive director, clinical hypotherapist, certified in Conversational Intelligence™ and Lifestyle Prescriptions®, and a licensed trainer of NLP™.

Cindy utilizes a knowledge of neuroscience and how the brain works to create change in individuals, management and sales teams that makes them happier and more successful in their professional and personal lives.

Her career is characterized by having regularly stepped outside the comfort zone to achieve milestones in the male-dominated nuclear fuel and energy brokerage and trading industries she worked in for decades.

Cindy was an investigative reporter in Chicago before moving to NYC to write about the nuclear industry. At 29, and having discovered a passion for markets, she helped launch a nuclear fuel brokerage company that revolutionized within months the way nuclear fuel was priced. She was one of few women in this industry at the time, the youngest person and the only woman to have started a business like this.

Cindy helped grow the company for over a decade before forming her own nuclear fuel consultancy. She provided analysis for government agencies and some of the world's largest nuclear utilities and fuel suppliers while writing articles on nuclear issues that were regularly published in business magazines and daily newspapers.

After moving to London in the late 1990s, she designed and launched an electricity newsletter for the world's second largest commodity price-reporting company and developed its coverage of European weather derivatives trading. She was appointed the company's first female managing editor and created the role of global managing editor, overseeing its largest and highest revenue-generating division.

Over time Cindy felt drawn to do something different. Knowing she wanted change was easy; figuring out what to do wasn't. The techniques she developed while creating the successful business she runs today, and her work with clients to do the same, are highlighted in her best-selling book, *"More to give-Stepping into your new life at any age."*

You Have The Power!

by Cindy Galvin

*"Day by day, what you choose, what you think and
what you do is who you become" -Heraclitus*

Early experiences mold a lifetime

I was five when I realized I was different.

It's when I first remember my sister telling me how ugly I was and she laughed at my 'funny' legs and 'ugly' orthopaedic shoes.

Some of what she said was true. There was one portrait of me in our home while there were many of her – the professional model. I'd been born with both legs doubled in half with my feet resting on the inside of each thigh. Casts put on my legs after birth straightened them while I grew, while at night I wore shoes affixed to a steel bar that forced my feet into the correct anatomical positions.

I was 17 when weekly visits to the podiatrist and the wearing of corrective shoes stopped. It coincided with leaving for university and sparked an incredible sense of freedom I'd never felt before. The external evidence of the defects had receded by then, but it would take years for the internal scars to heal.

I now view the birth defects as a gift because I developed early on an acute empathy for others and the drive to succeed. I vowed that nothing would hold me back. It's no surprise I've been drawn to roles that allowed me to travel the world and learn from the incredibly diverse people I met and worked with.

It's taken over 50 years for my passion for getting to know people and experiences to lead me in a different direction. I delight in the work I do today, teaching clients how to rewire their brains to achieve the happiest and most productive lives they can.

The gift of change

All of us are born with an amazing gift that enables us to create more happiness and fulfilment in our personal and professional lives. But many will never take advantage of this capability, even though it's free and there for the taking.

The gift I'm referring to is the ability to harness the power of your brain. This includes reframing your thoughts to think more positively, being mindful of your internal dialogue and noticing the words you use with others.

It's also recognizing that what you think impacts you. There is no stronger voice than our own that propels us forward to achieve what we want, and no stronger influence that will resolutely hold us back from doing so.

Making small changes in these areas will reduce stress, improve your health, boost confidence, help develop trust in work and personal relationships and, ultimately, change your life in ways you could never foresee.

I know from experience just how life-altering taking control of how you think and feel is. It's something I had to learn after leaving a successful career in my '50s to launch a new company in a field completely different to anything I'd done before. Despite having started two successful companies in the past, the task felt daunting. The confident woman I'd always been morphed into someone with more doubts and questions than answers. My insomnia and stress increased. Was I too old to start over? What if the business wasn't a success? More crucially, what exactly did I want to do?

After wasting time and money working with several advisors who promised great results that weren't delivered, I took things in hand. After a period of intensive study, I created my own techniques to confront and change negative thoughts and beliefs and grow my confidence, all of which allowed me to launch and build the successful business I run today.

My clients benefit from the mistakes I've made and the things I've learned as I help them create happier and more productive lives personally and professionally. I developed a five-step Platform for Success program to help those wanting to make career changes later in life achieve that goal. My experiences and clients' successes led me to write my best-selling book 'More to Give - Stepping into your new life at any age'.

I didn't consciously plan to take the journey that got me where I am today, but I'm grateful for having been born with an insatiable curiosity and the desire to leave the Midwestern city I was born in to travel the world and learn as much as I could from everyone I met and every experience I had.

An explosion of research in the fields of neuroscience has given us better insights into how the brain works, while studies in neuroplasticity have shown that our brains continue to learn and grow throughout our lives. Our brain forms new neural connections every day as we experience things. Despite long-held beliefs that our brain function inevitably declines as we age, the opposite is true, barring health issues, so long as we stay active. There's no reason to stop doing what you're doing over the age of 50, 60 or 70, if you don't want to.

This is a point I often make with clients who want to change direction for the rest of their working careers but have similar questions and doubts to mine. It's everyone's right to live the happiest and healthiest life they can, and everyone has the power to help themselves achieve this. There are more people working in their '60s', 70's and '80s now than ever before and this trend is set to continue.

5 Steps to Success

The five-step program I mentioned earlier guides clients from feeling stuck to envisioning and achieving their next goal be that a new career, a different job or launching a new business. I believe these five steps form the foundation for change. The five are **Clarity, Confidence, Commitment, Companions and Contribution.**

Clarity: You're unlikely to achieve your goal without being clear about what you want to do. It's like taking a road trip without having a map or GPS. You'll eventually get where you want to go, but it will take longer, and be more circuitous and painful, than if you'd followed a plan.

Confidence: You can have the best intentions to get what you want, but you won't achieve your goal if you're hesitant or lack confidence.

Commitment: You need a system that keeps you motivated and moving forward toward your dream.

Companions: A key aspect of success is your network. You need to identify the skills you don't have so you can methodically add to your network those who do have the talent you need and whose views differ from yours.

Contribution: Contribution is about giving back of your time or expertise. We feel more fulfilled and happier when we share with others. Giving back also increases the levels of the brain's 'feel good' chemicals that lighten and improve our mood.

When others say you can't, know you can

The act of thinking causes the brain to release neurotransmitters that talk to other parts of the brain and the nervous system. People who express gratitude every day enjoy a surge of the brain chemicals dopamine, oxytocin and serotonin that create feelings of euphoria, motivation, the feeling of belonging and concentration. What we think matters.

Our brains are hard-wired to default to negativity. This is because the oldest part, the reptilian brain, was programmed to be on alert for perceived danger. When danger is felt, the brain shuts down all resources except those needed to fight or run away.

Centuries of practice have created a strong negative, neural pathway that is reinforced with every negative thought or experience we have. Our thoughts are like hikers faced with two paths to take - one that's clear and easy to navigate and another thats overgrown and unused. Thoughts will always take the easy route.

307

To give you an idea of the impact this has on us, think of a situation where you've been praised for doing something well, won an award or came in first. Focus on what you saw, heard and felt at the time, to the best that you can. Now think of a time when you were criticized, shut down in conversations or reprimanded. Again, notice what you saw, heard and felt. You may notice the residual feeling from the negative experience is stronger than for the positive one.

Being aware of this brain activity is helpful in several ways. We run into negative people on a regular basis. Because of the way our brain works, we can be prone to take on critical comments others make, which affects us mentally and physiologically. Stop to realize that people say things based on their unique view of the world. Ask yourself what their perspective could be to say the things they do and remember that you have control over whether or not you allow their words to affect you.

When the brain senses danger, which receiving critical comments can do, it sends a signal to increase cortisol levels in your body. Higher cortisol levels increase stress, which is well known to lead to health problems. We also know that high cortisol levels are linked to a decrease in brain size and cognitive function, according to research with middle-aged participants published in an October 2018 edition of *Neurology*.

An effective exercise to be aware of your internal dialogue is to write down your thoughts over a two-day period. Take a break from doing this for a day or two and go back to review what you've written. You may be surprised at what you find and how repetitive your thoughts are.

Choose negative statements you feel are holding you back from doing what you want to do and reframe them. For example, 'I don't know what to do' becomes 'I don't know what to do yet'. Thinking 'I'm too old to start over' can be 'I have decades of experience I bring to whatever I decide to do'. 'I'm always a failure' could be 'I learn from every mistake I make.'

The more aware you are of your internal thought patterns, the easier it will become to notice and change negative thoughts. Doing this also helps you build a more positive neural pathway.

Words Create Worlds

I help clients learn coping strategies to deal with the physical and mental strain of competitiveness, long hours and game playing that exist in stressful work environments. I have occasionally worked in situations like this myself and wish I'd known techniques to feel less belittled from constant criticism and verbal bullying from managers.

One of the most important elements of being a good manager is to listen. Dr. Judith E. Glaser, the creator of Conversational Intelligence™(C-IQ) calls this listening to connect. Broadly speaking this is listening to what someone else is saying without focusing on what you want to say in response.

C-IQ is about understanding how the way we talk with each other can lead to a shutdown in communication or open the door to cooperation. Glaser's work is based on insights from the latest neuroscience research showing which conversations trigger the reptilian brain to shut down and which activate parts of the brain that allow us to feel trust, empathy and the desire to work together. Put another way, the words we use with each other directly impact our brain chemicals and, in turn, how we interact with each other.

I am one of roughly 200 people certified in C-IQ training, and I use its tools with CEOs, senior managers and management and sales teams. I find it particularly effective for increasing trust and the desire to work together with teams created through merger and acquisition activity. The improvements in teamwork and collaboration directly impacts the company's bottom line.

The art of self-healing

'Whatever the mind can conceive and believe, it can achieve.'
                                    - Napoleon Hill

No discussion of changing your life can be complete without addressing health. You can be happy and have the best career in the world, but it will mean little if you suffer from chronic illness or other medical conditions.

An April 2016 Harvard Health blog on the psychology of back pain noted that people who feel they won't get better, and are anxious about their health, will make the pain worse. When pain lingers, it causes the brain to shift to the part that processes emotion. Eventually, controlling the emotion associated with the health issue is more difficult to do. What we think matters!

We are not victims of random illness because our symptoms are part of a meaningful biological process in our body. Over 80% of all chronic illnesses are caused by unresolved emotional issues. By eliminating the root cause triggers of these emotions, and the emotions themselves, you kickstart the body's natural healing process. This is part of the Lifestyle Prescriptions work that I do with clients and the results are amazing.

Over to You

You have the ability to take charge of your life and now have examples of how to start. It's your decision about whether you'll take advantage of them, but can you afford to waste more time?

I suspect some of you think you're too busy, stressed or time-pressed to fit something new into your schedule. Or maybe you feel you've tried similar exercises in the past to no avail.

I would argue that you can't let any opportunity to significantly improve your life pass you by. The changes become easier and are in proportion to your level of commitment.

Some of my clients have expected immediate change after investing a relatively short amount of time and feel the work has failed if this doesn't happen. Things move fast today and people expect this pace to be consistent in all areas of their lives. But when I mention the need to commit, I'm not talking years. I'm suggesting micro changes that can be done daily. The difference you begin to feel may surprise you.

Some things can be changed quickly and others can't. I've used NLP techniques to help people overcome fears and phobias in less than 10 minutes, but this is change in one particular area. Do you feel constrained from doing what you want? Would you like coping strategies to deal with work-place bullies, feelings of inadequacy, anxiety or being overwhelmed? These issues will take longer than 10 minutes to shift, but once done the results are lasting.

If you've ever wished life could be different, do something about it now. The resiliently successful and time-pressed clients I work with are amazed at the transformation they achieve by committing time and energy to making the mental shifts necessary to get the benefits they want. There's every reason you should believe a similar commitment will bring you the best life has to offer.

* * *

Cindy Galvin
www.cindygalvin.com
cindy@cindygalvin.com
+44 (0)207 4355325

Pat Sampson

Founder/Editor

America's Leading Ladies

ALLPress. Global

Pat Sampson

BIOGRAPHY

Pat Sampson's story is rooted in the good fortune of working for legendary sales executives many moons ago. "Think and Grow Rich" by Napoleon Hill was required reading, positive thinking seminars part of daily life.

This kind of thinking became her lifeline. A single mother and sole support of two little girls, Pat was motivated by the earning potential of salespeople to join one of the nation's leading community builders - and with no previous sales experience - ranked first in a 30,000 male-dominated sales force. After achieving the company's highest honors, she sought new challenges in the field of life insurance. Within six months she became the first woman in the company's 96-year history to achieve Four Honor Club Status; breaking into the exclusive One Hundred Million Dollar Sales Club in One Hundred Days.

Pat's astounding story - single mother $50 a week secretary - to six figures a year as one of the most prominent salespeople in the nation was featured in newspapers, magazines, and television. Thousands responded wanting to share their stories of challenges and success. This was the spark that ignited a dream that would never burn out. At the height of her career, she left substantial financial rewards behind to begin a most unrealistic journey: *to create a publishing company to honor entrepreneurs* - those passionate and purposeful risk takers - by publishing their stories to inspire others with a sense of what is possible.

A Journey of dreams - thirty years and counting - met with storms of challenges along the way but with the tireless faith and eternal optimism of a true believer, Pat believed in its power to become a beacon of hope and inspiration to people everywhere.

Credits: A Star to Steer By; Dreaming & Winning in America; Solid Goal: The Magazine for Winners; Positive News: A Good News Tabloid; The Power of Positive People; RE/MAX: A World of Winners; Leaders & Legends, America's STAR Entrepreneurs; and *America's Leading Ladies:* Ebook & Print. To connect as many kindred spirits as possible, launching any day www.networkofstars.com

A Journey of Dreams

by Pat Sampson

*"I am not afraid of storms, for I am learning
how to steer my ship." - Louise May Alcott*

Your dream will seek you out. It will become such an intimate part of you that it can never be denied. It will insist repeatedly that you begin it, and refuse to release you until you complete it. Only then have you found your dream; waiting your touch to bring its greatness to life. Nothing great ever comes easy. All the storms you encounter along the way eventually blow away.

When the waters of circumstances come swirling about, jostling you to-and-fro, throwing you off balance and threatening to sweep you beneath its icy currents, *it is time to ride the tide.* The tide is not unfriendly, for it is responsive to the heavens itself as it surges toward its destination. Its breakers cannot be swept backward and subdued, any more than life itself can be captured and bottled - as we sail emotional seas, fight mental battles, and make spiritual progress, and warned to turn back by travelers who believe the voyage impossible.

Sail On! for happiness is guaranteed the soul who refuses to hesitate or turn back. Choose carefully your crew and traveling companions. You may find the currents intense, and sometimes fierce, but faced head-on and braved, leaves you worthier, stronger, wiser, and more confident than before; having won the admiration and respect of those who wish to be like you.

There are no highways at sea. When you leave the comfortable familiarity of the harbor, you move into a wide-open, ever-changing world. Perspectives are altered, distances become harder to gauge and landmarks along the shore take on new and often perplexing aspects. In order to keep track of your destination, you must learn to navigate successfully.

The universe is governed by certain immutable laws, from the balance of a seagull's wings, the warmth of the sun, the radiance of the moon, the waves in the ocean: all are responsive to the basic principles of life, the greatest of which is the power of creation. Creation responds to the impetus of belief as it does to no other thing. Always keep a reserve supply deep within your heart. Although you may be operating in a dense fog of seemingly impossible circumstances, you will feel a comforting sense of knowing exactly where you are.

Believe in yourself. You may not know what others will do, but you know what you believe in, what you trust, what you think is right. Listen to clues from your emotions to guide you. A lack of enthusiasm speaks the need for excitement or a renewed sense of purpose; an inner longing may mean a talent awaits development and needs more channels of expression. Never give up on your dreams, even when nobody else believes it can come true but you.

The Destroyer Fear will always appear when it is time to change course. She will threaten you with torpedoes of uncertainty; fire cannons of doubt; and besiege you with negativism. She will create illusions of danger where there are none. She will magnify circumstances out of proportion, making small ice-floes seem like glaciers, too monumental to approach, let alone overcome . These same obstacles, viewed by the light of self-confidence, shrink, melt and disappear.

Be on guard for fear. She may attempt to disguise herself as caution or practicality. She may travel under the ruse of maturity or fly the flag of security, but she is anything but secure. Fear is the height of insecurity. If you summon even a little confidence she will quickly turn and flee. Each time you win a victory over fear, your beacons of confidence become a little brighter, a little more intense, until eventually they crystalize into a radiant light beaming from a watchtower of courage. Other travelers will recognize that light and feel safer in your passing, while the Destroyer Fear will dare not travel the same seas.

As a child of the universe, you are protected, you are loved. You are no less a miracle than the seas you travel, or the skies under which you sail. You are endowed with the ability to create for yourself any life of which you feel capable. Destiny waits to do your bidding. At your fingertips is the power of creation. You must answer to the now, realizing the spirituality that lies beneath all things using each moment to bring it creatively alive. Always bearing in mind - you are charting a course that someone else may follow.

The very light whose reflection lighted the way for your arrival will now become a part of you and you will fulfill the highest and noblest aim of any human being - **to light the way for others.**

* * *

Pat Sampson, Founder & Editor
America's Leading Ladies
ALLPress.Global@gmail.com
www.networkofstars.com
networkofstars11@gmail.com

"You have
to find
what sparks
a light in you
so that you
in your own way
can illuminate
the world."

- Oprah Winfrey

The environment
is where we
all meet;
where all have
a mutual interest;
it is the one thing
all of us share.

-Lady Bird Johnson